Intentional Leadership

Your path to becoming the kind of leader people respect, follow, and love to work with

by
John Stange

© John Stange, 2016
All Rights Reserved

~ *Ivystream Press* ~
Philadelphia, Pennsylvania

To contact the author or learn about his other books and resources, please visit
DesireJesus.com *or* **JohnStange.com**

Scripture quotations are from The Holy Bible, English Standard Version® (ESV®), copyright © 2001 by Crossway, a publishing ministry of Good News Publishers. Used by permission. All rights reserved.

No part of this book or any of its contents may be reproduced, copied, modified or adapted, without the prior written consent of the author, unless otherwise indicated for stand-alone materials.

Table of Contents

Chapter 1 - My Leadership Journey...7
Chapter 2 - Influence vs. Positional Leadership.........................13
Chapter 3 - Unleashing Creativity..17
Chapter 4 - Emotional Drain...23
Chapter 5 - My Favorite Form of Revenge................................29
Chapter 6 - Your Identity is Not what you Do..........................33
Chapter 7 - Taking Action and Gaining Respect......................39
Chapter 8 - The Greatest Leaders are Servants.........................45
Chapter 9 - Three words every leader needs to say..................51
Chapter 10 - Will you Run or Will you Grow?.........................55
Chapter 11 - Why do Good Leaders Mentor Others?..............59
Chapter 12 - What is your Level of Teachability?....................65
Chapter 13 - Unrealistic Expectations...71
Chapter 14 - Overcome your Fear of Public Speaking.............77
Chapter 15 - How to not be a Failure..83
Chapter 16 - Personal Finances..89
Chapter 17 - Leading through Seasons of Change...................97
Chapter 18 - Motivation and Appreciation..............................105
Chapter 19 - Questions and Answers..111
Wrapping Up - 117
Contact the Author - 119

Chapter 1

My Leadership Journey

Leadership is an interesting role. For many people, I would imagine that being a "leader" sounds glamorous, fun and filled with perks. Real leaders know that that isn't always necessarily the case. True leaders often make great sacrifices that others will never be aware of. Yes, they may enjoy serving in their role, but they also know that good leaders have the heart of a servant and a willingness to remain committed to the cause regardless of the setback, criticism or opposition they may receive along the way.

I have had the privilege of observing both sides of leadership, the glamorous side and the torturous side, my entire life. When I was a child, my family owned and ran a grocery store. The business was started by my great-grandfather, continued by my grandfather who then sold it to my father and my uncle who expanded the business into three stores.

Growing up, I looked up to the men in my family. I was used to seeing them in charge. I regularly watched them give quality people jobs while also firing dishonest employees. I felt a genuine sense of pride when it came to our family business and I learned a lot by working with my father, grandfather and uncle, as well as with the other employees they hired to be part of their team.

The opportunity to work at the store started early in our family. Because I wanted to be just like my Dad and the rest of the family, I begged him to let me work at the store when I was five-years-old. And I had two specific requests for my first day at work. I wanted to wear an apron like he did when he was working in the meat department AND I wanted to get paid with a check. He granted my request and from the time I was in kindergarten, I worked at the store regularly.

In time, I stocked shelves, sliced meat, worked the register, made deliveries and (my least favorite task) cleaned the meat department at the end of the day. That task was rather gross, to be honest.

All the while, I was observing my father and the rest of my family. My Dad was the boss. Everything ran through him. He had a good team of employees, but he called the shots. It was a fun environment to learn the ins and outs of leadership. And even though I was his son, he made a point to insist that I never received special treatment in that environment. He didn't want me acting like an entitled brat just because my last name was on the sign and to be honest, he held me to a higher standard of ethics and work performance than he did the rest of the employees. Sometimes, in the moment, that would irritate me, but I'm very grateful for what that experience taught me in the long run. Many of the patterns and approaches that I take toward leadership were forged in that environment.

During the Summer, I also worked at a camp that was affiliated with my church. I loved camping there as a child and applied to be on the Summer staff just before I turned fifteen. I could write a book about that experience alone (and maybe someday I will), but the Summer I first worked on the staff was the pivotal moment of my entire life. I often tell my own children that the person they know me to be today was born through the experience I had working at camp.

It was through that experience that I became serious about my faith in Jesus Christ. I also developed some of the closest and longest lasting friendships of my life.

I came back to work at that camp year after year and I was gradually promoted through the ranks. I started by working on the grounds crew, then I was promoted to work in the snack shop. The following year, I was hired as a cabin counselor and groups of children and teens were placed under my leadership. That position truly stretched me. It was difficult, but I started to understand what leadership felt like and what my unique leadership style happened to be.

After several years as a counselor, I was promoted to the position of Program Director. My job was to put together the schedule of activities for the Summer and to lead the staff in implementing the program. In later years, I was asked to serve on the Board of Directors and eventually, I was hired as the year-round Director of the camp. All aspects of the camp were placed under my leadership and oversight. I was in charge of hiring, firing, promotion, retreats, building, repairing and building teams of people that would help me implement each of these tasks. I can honestly say that I have never had a harder job. But I loved it.

At the same time, I was also pastoring a church. While I was in college, I was hired as a youth director at a church not too far from where I was studying. The job was difficult, but also a lot of fun. After a year or so in that position, the pastor started asking me to preach for him on Sundays when he was away. I was nervous about that thought, but I agreed and once I got the hang of it, I realized how much I loved it. I had been going to college to become a history teacher, but gradually came to realize that my interests had transitioned to pastoral ministry.

I had been dating a girl at the time. Her name was Andrea and she was also an education major. She helped me with the youth group and we were convinced that we were going to get married. She thought she was about to marry a high-school history teacher, but as it was becoming clear to me that I was going to become a pastor, I asked her what she thought about that. To my relief, she was enthusiastic about that idea. We dated for a little over three years and the day after I finished college, we got married. A week later, I was hired by my first church and three weeks after that, we moved to western Pennsylvania where my pastoral ministry began.

I served that church for a year and was re-stationed by my denomination to another church near where I grew up the next year. That decision was outside of my control, but to be honest, I was glad they moved me. The church they moved me had been pastored by a man that I really looked up to and he was retiring. I had been a guest speaker at the church on occasion in the past and both he and I could tell that we would be a good match. When he retired, the church leadership requested that I be transferred there and the committee that was in charge of that agreed that it was a good fit so we moved.

I served that church for eight years. The community had been established by coal companies in the 1800's and the town still had somewhat of a hard edge to it, which I strangely appreciated and often enjoyed. I loved the people of that church and many of them were very supportive of my leadership. There were also a few people in that church that typically gave pastors a difficult time, but I learned the importance of standing up to "church bullies" in that context and ironically, I noticed that after I confronted some of these bullies, their respect for me seemed to grow and they didn't cause quite as much trouble within the church.

The church also supported me when I was asked to direct the camp. The camp was about 45 minutes away from the church and I would drive back and forth between both places most days. But thankfully, the church family supported me in this task and many people of all ages got on board with helping as they could with the needs of the camp.

In time, it became clear to me that I couldn't keep running at that pace. Leading both ministries at the same time wasn't sustainable long term. Both the church and the camp were growing, but I was starting to burn out. During this time, Andrea and I also had four children, close in age. I was certain that if I tried to lead both ministries, my family would pay too great a price, so I decided that I needed to pick one and step down from the other.

After a lot of prayer and discussion, I became convinced that I needed to step down from the church. I was feeling a strong tug to get involved in "church planting", which is the process of starting brand new churches, and I was convinced that the Lord was eventually going to lead me in that direction. So I gave the church almost a year's notice, and at the end of that year, I stepped down. One year later, I also stepped down from serving as the Director of the camp and I moved my family to the Philadelphia region to re-plant a church where one had just died.

Since that time, I have been pastoring this church. We started with about six people and over the years, we have watched the church gradually grow into a healthy family. One of the areas that I have focused on during this season of my leadership is the concept of "leadership development." I have been assembling a team of leaders and ministry directors to oversee all aspects of this ministry. My wife doesn't like when I say this, but my long-term goal is that if I ever get hit by a truck, this church can continue on without me because the right leadership and vision is in place to facilitate this ministry long after I'm gone.

There are other hats I wear in addition to my pastoral

role, but I won't bore you with the rest of those details. I wanted to share a little bit about my leadership journey at the start of this book because it is relevant to the concepts found in the rest of this book.

The process of becoming a leader isn't easy. I have learned many painful lessons along the way and I'm still in the process learning new lessons. I believe that leadership development is a life-long process and something that we always need to remain intentionally invested in. Good leadership skills and practices don't come about by accident. They are the result of intentional decisions being made all along the way.

Are you in a position of leadership or do you anticipate being placed in one? How can you become the kind of leader that others enjoy working with? What traits are present in the lives of good leaders? What beliefs and practices should you be committed to if you want to be intentional about leading others well?

In the coming chapters, I'm going to share some of the major lessons I have learned along the way. Because I'm still in the process of learning and growing, it wouldn't surprise me if someday I add a few more chapters to this book, but at present, this is a collection of some of what I have gathered over the course of the past few decades of my life and leadership.

Thank you for allowing me to share this with you. I sincerely hope that it's helpful and truly believe that it will be.

Chapter 2

Influence vs. Positional Leadership

What is the essence of leadership?

What do many people mistakenly confuse leadership to be?

What is the difference between "influence" and "positional leadership"?

Not long ago, I was reading parts of the book, *"The 21 Irrefutable Laws of Leadership"* by John Maxwell to my children. It probably seems odd that I would read a book like that to four kids, but it's a great book and I like sharing things with them that I believe will be truly helpful to them in life.

One of the comments John Maxwell makes in that book is that "Leadership is influence, nothing more, nothing less." His point is that if you have influence over others, you are in a position where you are leading them to some degree, whether you can lay claim to a formal title or not.

More often than not, people tend to think of leadership as being positional in nature. Meaning, if I have a title that has been bestowed on me from someone else, then somehow that makes me a leader. And in some respect, I can see how that can be interpreted as the case, but real leadership isn't found in a title or in pushing people to do what they don't want to do. Real leadership is "influence" that is strong enough to effectively invite people to join you in what you're doing.

Think for a moment about two categories of people in your life. Bosses or managers that you've worked for and taken orders from and people who have had a major influence on you.

Who do you feel more loyal to? Who do you admire more? Who has made a more profound impact on your life? Which category of leader has impacted your perspective, the way you speak, the way you treat your spouse or your children, the way you conduct yourself in public, they way you dress, etc.?

A leader who operates in a role that is only positional in nature, often has very little lasting influence. And influence is the essence of leadership, so that means that positional leadership often means that a person who has a title may not actually be much of a leader at all.

I think we can all bring to memory some people who thought they were leaders just because they had a title. And we can also think of people that truly were leaders even though they had no title whatsoever.

I used this example when I was speaking with my 9 year old daughter, Julia, recently. I asked her if she thought she was a leader and her first response was that she really didn't think she was. Then I asked her to consider all the people she has an influence on.

Julia is a very outgoing and caring child. She genuinely likes people and she doesn't have much fear in meeting new people, young or old. She doesn't hesitate to interject herself into the lives of others, and people genuinely like her.

This past Summer, all my kids camped at Summer Camp. They camp at the same camp I used to attend as a child and later directed as an adult. Julia invited some of her friends to go and they decided to go, even though they're young and have never been away from home like that before. They wanted to go because Julia was going to be there. In fact, the camp director told us that in addition to those kids, there were other kids who specifically requested on their registration forms to be in Julia's cabin. The cabins can only hold so many campers and it turned out that more kids wanted to be in Julia's cabin than could actually fit.

I reminded her of that and I asked her again to think about whether or not she was a leader. I wanted her to see that she has a powerful influence on many of her friends and I encouraged her to continue using that to bless the lives of other people. Again, as John Maxwell states, "Leadership is influence, nothing more, nothing less." If people willingly accept you as an influence in their life, you are a leader whether you set out to be or not.

So let me throw the question out there. Who do you influence? Who is making decisions based on what they learn from you or observe in your life? Who is copying you? Who seeks and accepts your counsel?

You don't need a title to lead. Frankly, some of the worst leaders I have ever encountered were people who leaned almost exclusively on the fact that they had a title when they tried to lead others. They may have "bossed" others, but they certainly weren't "leading" them in the truest sense.

My sons cracked me up last week. They were going to visit family with my wife and I couldn't go with them, so I reminded them to all be good for their mother while they were in the van. (This is a healthy and necessary reminder for a van full of children).

My 11-year-old son, Daniel, asked me before they left to put him in charge of his siblings, so I joking said, sure. But then he asked me to announce that to the family before they drove away, so I jokingly announced it. Jay, my 13-year-old son didn't like the thought of his younger brother being in charge so at first he let out an audible, "Awwww."

But then something dawned on him from what I had been reading to them and he blurted out, "Wait! Daniel is just a positional leader! True leadership is influence!" That cracked me up and I loved watching that lesson sink in a little deeper into their minds and experiences.

So, again, I don't know what role you play in leadership, but keep in mind that the essence of real leadership isn't found in a title, a position or a role. True leadership is seen in those who influence others.

If you are an influencer, even on the smallest of scales, you are a leader and I would encourage you to value your role and use it to bless those who look to you for leadership. You've been give a real privilege and with that privilege comes responsibility. Use your influence well and don't rely on titles as a leadership crutch because a title doesn't automatically equate to leadership.

Chapter 3

Unleashing creativity and personal investment from your team

What does it look like to unleash and encourage creativity within your team?

How can you encourage your team to become personally invested in the mission of your organization?

Not long ago, I experienced several good reminders about what it takes to encourage your team to employ creativity AND how giving them opportunities to do so can have the residual effect of increasing their level of personal investment in your organization.

To set this up, let me share a few things that are often character traits in organizational leaders. Organizational leaders are typically people that are both vision oriented and people centered. That can be a delicate balance to try to maintain and depending on how strongly you feel about your personal vision, it can be easy at times to push people away while you're trying to implement your vision, even though deep down you know and you want others to be joining you in the process.

Sometimes, a leader can get a vision in their mind and then push forward for the implementation of that vision according to very exact standards. It certain moments, that's totally fine, but in other contexts, that needs to be done carefully, particularly if you're also trying to encourage your team to adopt your vision and join you in your mission.

If you push certain aspects of your vision in the wrong way, you can unintentionally discourage or exasperate your team. And if that continues for too long of a period of time, you can end up chasing your team away. They'll stop following your leadership because you've become more of a boss than a leader.

Your vision has value, but if you can be a little flexible with it, it can be greatly enhanced by the ideas and creativity of your team. For some leaders, that can be a tricky balance to try to strike because they might fear that the implementation of their vision might end up being changed or altered too much from what they truly think is best for the organization.

But that's a risk you'll often have to take and to be honest, there can also be benefits that come from moments when ideas are given permission to be tried and then those ideas are shown not to be effective.

What I'm getting at is this.... If you are convinced that you have the right people on your team (and that's key), you should make a habit of trusting them when they offer creative suggestions and offer to implement those suggestions for the betterment of the organization. Again, if you have the right people on your team and they share your overall values and goals, letting them use their creativity can be a great blessing to your organization and it can likewise increase their level of loyalty and personal investment.

Let me give you two examples from my life that reminded me of this recently.

1. **Bonfire / Movie**

Not long ago, our church hosted a bonfire and showed an outdoor movie at the back of our parking lot. This was, of all places, in a retention basin on the edge of our property.

The idea was first suggested to me by one of the men in the church and to be honest, when he first brought it up, I wasn't completely sold. I wasn't opposed to the idea, but I couldn't help but wonder if he was setting himself up for disappointment. In my mind I thought, "Why would people come to an outdoor movie on a chilly Fall night, and watch that movie in a retention basin behind our church when they could just watch a movie in the comfort of their home on a big screen TV?" It seemed to me like the kind of event that might have worked well 15 or 20 years ago, but not so much today.

But I didn't want to stifle this man's idea because I was really just going off of my opinion, so I gave the green light for it and he along with a couple other people worked hard to pull it off. I helped promote it, but they made it happen and they did a great job. In fact, it was really well attended and for the past few days, people have been mentioning to me how much they loved it and how they hope we do it again next October. We even had a bunch of families from the neighborhood around the church come and bring their kids. I was impressed.

So what are the takeaways from that?

- We unleashed this man's creativity by giving him permission to act on an idea that he had.
- He very much supports our mission and vision as an organization and is a quality guy, so we have every reason to trust his judgment.
- The event went well and he was encouraged.

- This has strengthened his loyalty and personal investment in our organization because we trusted him and gave him an opportunity to succeed.

Let me give you another example that took place recently in our church.

2. Ministry Director Booths

Our church is only a few years old. We began the work of planting it in 2008, but the formal launch and grand opening was in September of 2010. Since that time, we have been trying to identify leaders and place them in key roles according to their gifts, preferences, ability and track record. We call this team of leaders our Ministry Directors and they oversee key functions of the church like; children's ministries, sound and technology, congregational care, hospitality, greeting, building care, etc.

I tell the Ministry Directors all the time that they are "my team" and that I want them to be building their team. That means that I want our Nursery Director to be building and assembling a team of volunteers that work with her to provide nursery care, I want the Music Director to be building a team of musicians that work with him, I want the Building & Property Director to be building a team that works with him, etc. And that's what they've been doing. Teams are growing and the church is growing healthier as a result.

At our last meeting, our Congregational Care Director who is also now our Church Administrator suggested an idea. She thought it would be good for our Ministry Directors to have a Sunday where they all set up booths in the church to highlight their ministries and encourage people to sign up to be on a team that fit with their talents and gifting.

I had no idea if this would work and deep down, I feared that our MD's would set up booths and people would walk right by them, but I gave the green light and they set up booths for people to visit. I encouraged the congregation at both of our worship services to stop by these booths and, if nothing else, thank our MD's for the great work they do to bless our church family. I was pleasantly surprised to see just how many people stopped by and even more pleased to learn that many of our MD's were able to add more members to their teams. The idea worked great.

So what are the takeaways from that?

- We unleashed this woman's creativity by giving her permission to organize and implement her idea.
- She very much supports our mission and vision as an organization and is a quality person, so we have every reason to trust her judgment.
- The event went well and she was encouraged.
- This has strengthened her loyalty and personal investment in our organization because we trusted her and gave her an opportunity to succeed.

One other takeaway that I think is key in both of these examples. Even though I didn't know ahead of time if these ideas would work, I knew it was important for me as the most visible leader to actively support the creativity of our team. I wanted them to know that I was behind them, win or lose. Truthfully, I would much rather us regularly try new things as an organization than to grow stale by getting into a rut simply because we're afraid of failure.

Not trying something new would be a failure. I don't

consider it a failure to try to implement a creative idea from a trusted member of our team. Even if it didn't work they way we hoped, at least we could learn something for next time AND they can be assured that their leader stood behind them and their attempt to make the organization better.

Embrace your team's creativity. Let people you trust attempt to make your organization better. Every good idea doesn't have to come from you. Celebrate their success. You'll encourage your team, bless your organization and help your co-leaders develop a deeper sense of loyalty to your mission, vision and leadership.

Chapter 4

Emotional Drain - The most difficult aspect of leadership?

What do you enjoy most about leadership?

What do think many seasoned leaders consider the most difficult aspect of leadership?

How does becoming aware of what drains us of the joy of serving in our role of leadership help us last longer and resist burning out?

If you have risen to the rank of leader in whatever sphere you operate in, the corporate world, manufacturing, education, ministry, etc., odds are you're someone who cares deeply about what you do. You have likely spent years training and learning so that you can do what you do well. You probably have a great track record that has been observable over a longer period of time.

And long before you even had the opportunity to work or train in your occupation, you probably spent time dreaming about it. You imagined what it would be like to serve in your field. For years, you probably observed other leaders and thought, "If I ever have the opportunity to lead, I'll do it this way or that way."

I imagine that you've also demonstrated loyalty to your company or organization and it has probably puzzled you to observe others who haven't been loyal. Now, you're in the position of leadership and all the things that you used to daydream about are things that you're actually doing. All the things you trained for are now the responsibilities that you've been entrusted to handle. All the people you observed during your formative years come back to your mind as you have the responsibility to make decisions in your organization.

But, if you've been leading long enough, you've probably also experienced fatigue. Maybe the energy you used to have for your role just isn't there. Maybe it seems somewhat comical to you to think that you used to daydream about doing what you're doing now.

What's the problem? Why do you feel so drained or exhausted? What's eating at you?

This isn't universally true, but many roles of leadership aren't physically exhausting. Many leaders do a large percentage of their leading from a desk, a board room or a lunch table. It isn't necessarily physically exhausting to meet with team members, make strategic plans, talk on the phone, place orders, read spreadsheets, etc.

Likewise, many roles of leadership aren't necessarily mentally exhausting. If you're an engineer, I'm sure you find many aspects of your work to be mentally stimulating. If you're a professor, you're probably fascinated by some of the subjects you research and teach. If you're a pastor, you probably feel highly enlightened by your study of Scripture and probably consider it a privilege to experience the personal growth that comes through the time you spend in message preparation.

So what is it about leadership roles that often make them so draining? If it isn't the physical exhaustion or the mental exhaustion, where is the drain coming from? For many of us, the drain is emotional in nature.

What does that look like? Well, if you're a leader, that means that your primary task isn't working with data or working with things, it's working with people. And people can be complicated, as any leader can attest.

Some people are easy to lead. They're teachable, supportive, encouraging and loyal. They share your values and vision and they genuinely like you (and odds are, you genuinely like them.)

But then there are others who may not be so easy to lead. They come to work with a chip on their shoulder. You know they probably question many of your decisions. You also probably know that they need you to keep an eye on them to guarantee that they do the job they're supposed to do.

At the same time you're dealing with people and their personalities and preferences, you're also trying to think ahead strategically regarding your organization. You're making plans and you're implementing vision. You're also doing your best to make sure that everything is running correctly from personnel, to suppliers, to machinery, to utilities, to furnaces and so on.

Many leaders come to realize that they really never get to completely "clock out." The organization you lead is ALWAYS on your mind. The people, the moving parts, the momentum or lack of momentum. You're always thinking about it and before you know it, you feel tapped. You may even feel anxious.

- Have you ever struggled to sleep at night because of your role of leadership?
- Have you ever had a day off or a vacation interrupted with thoughts of or communication with your organization?
- Have you ever had to drive back to your place of work

at an odd hour to handle something that had to be handled by you because you're the primary leader?

For five years, I led an organization called PMBC, the Pocono Mountain Bible Conference. It is the conference center and a Summer camp that I mentioned in Chapter 1. Its program runs all year in the beautiful Pocono Mountains of Northeast, Pennsylvania.

In addition to the staff, the marketing, and the support raising, the buildings and property were always on my mind. Winters are harsh there. Pipes freeze and break. Furnaces quit. The pool breaks. The ice machine breaks. Roofs leak. Trees fall down. Other things break. There is a lot that the Director of PMBC is responsible to oversee and the emotional drain that comes with always having the care of the facilities (as well as the needs of the staff) on your mind can be heavy.

I remember one evening when I was shopping at Walmart. I was feeling emotionally and physically tired at the time. I remember daydreaming for a moment as the cashier rang up my items and thinking, *"I wish I had her job. She clocks in at a set time and clocks out at a set time. She doesn't have to worry about deliveries and if they come on time or if the heating system in this building works. When she leaves this place, she doesn't have to think about her job again until she comes back. AND, she probably gets a few days off each week where work is the furthest thing from her mind."*

Now obviously, I was drained because I'm sure a cashier at Walmart can tell me about all the things they have to do for their job that are quite unsavory, but in that moment, it seemed to me like she had the best job in the world and I wanted it. I wanted to work the cash register. I didn't want to lead or give orders. I wanted to take orders, at least for a season. I wanted the emotional weight of being the "point person" released from weighing me down.

I don't know if you're going through a season like that right now or not, but if you are, please allow me to ask a few questions and offer a few ideas that seem to help me when I find myself in that spot.

- 1. Are you building a team of people that you like and trust that can help shoulder your burdens? If you are, great. A team of specialists is more effective than one generalist and a shared burden is lighter for all parties.
- 2. Do you have an unhealthy sense of your importance? If you do, it's time to acknowledge it so you can move into a healthier perspective on your role and contribution to your organization.
- 3. Have you become addicted to your work OR addicted to winning the approval of others in the context of your organization, to the point that you're sacrificing your emotional well-being?
- 4. Would you be willing to structure time off in such a way that you can truly get away AND give yourself permission to not worry about the consequences of your absence? So what if the furnace breaks. So what if someone quits. So what if your team plots a coup to overthrow you in your absence.

I know for me that I have had to ask these questions and make some changes to my routine to help combat the emotional fatigue I sometimes experience. I have needed and continue to need to:

- Build my team

- Trust my team and avoid micromanaging them
- Schedule quarterly time off including a 2 week stretch right after Christmas.
- Give myself permission to enjoy a few healthy distractions (movies, kayaking, long drives, etc.)

Good leadership is needed in this world and if you're a good leader, you need to take some time to care for yourself with the kind of energy and enthusiasm that you often show toward your people and your organization. Everyone wins if you're healthy, rested and encouraged.

Don't feel guilty about it. Don't feed your anxiety in the process. Just give yourself an emotional break and make giving yourself emotional breaks a regular part of your routine so that you can be an emotionally healthy leader who lasts in your role of leadership for a long time without burning out.

Chapter 5

My favorite form of revenge

In just a few moments, I'm going to share with you my favorite form of revenge. Now, this probably doesn't sound like a very "pastoral" thing for me to be speaking about, but I'm not going to lie, I take this form of revenge whenever I can.

I know that might sound odd or unhealthy, but before you judge me too harshly, I know this is something that you've thought about too. If you're a leader, there are people out there who have annoyed and upset you - people that have been abrasive and unkind. People who have hurt you, criticized you and people who have made your life more difficult that you feel it needed to be. So what's a great way to get revenge on these people?

Years ago when I was new to leadership and was early in my work as a pastor, I came across one of the most abrasive, unkind and unreasonable people I ever met. He had a knack for upsetting just about everyone in his life and in our church.

I'll never forget one Sunday when, through his mean spirit and hurtful words, he made several women in the church cry. I didn't witness it with my own eyes, but of course I received calls and second hand information about it. I remember thinking, "Oh great. That guy is a piece of work and now I'm going to have to confront him about his actions toward the women of the church."

That happened on a Sunday. I received calls about him later that day and decided that I would try to set up a meeting with him the next day. I called his house on Monday and he wasn't there, but his wife took the message and said she would have him call me when he got back from work. Fine. No problem.

In the meantime, my wife went to the doctor for a pregnancy visit. She was coming close to the due date for our first child and this was her last scheduled visit before the birth. While I was waiting for the return call from the man who was causing trouble, I got a call from her saying that she wasn't coming home. Her doctor told her to get to the hospital because the baby was on the way.

Oh great. My first child is about to be born and I'm in my office waiting for a return call from someone I need to confront.

Right after I spoke to my wife, I got the call, chatted with him briefly and cautioned him to be more mindful of his behavior, then left for the hospital to be with my wife and later that day we celebrated the birth of our daughter.

That man behaved himself for a while, but then got riled up again over something new. And because I was one of the few people in his life that didn't cower from him, he started trying to act all tough around me. He would come to the church earlier than anyone on Sunday mornings, sit in his seat and not say a word. He'd just sit there in an empty building with his family next to him and he wouldn't speak. But I'd still walk up to him each week, greet him politely and say, "Good morning, Mr. So & So."
He wouldn't say a word.

I did this week after week. Month after month. Nothing.

Not a word from him. Finally, one Sunday, I just wasn't in the mood for him so I walked right past him and didn't say hello. I just didn't feel like it that day. But for whatever reason, I didn't like how that made me feel. He could be a jerk all he wanted. There wasn't much I could do about that. But I didn't want to join him in that. I didn't want to be a jerk too. So I went back to saying hello to him.

That was my revenge. I was kind to him even though he wasn't kind to me. I was honest, upfront and reasonable with him, even though he didn't act in good faith or logic toward me.

I had another experience with some similarities not too long ago. A man who lives in my neighborhood has a child that likes to play with my children, except his child is often rude, selfish and uses more foul language than most adults I know.

My children usually shy away from playing with him because he can be hard to deal with and he usually runs home and tells his dad how all the other kids in the neighborhood are being mean to him. Then his dad gets angry and starts trouble with the other parents. I hadn't experienced the dad's wrath yet, but my day finally came.

He showed up at my door and started reaming me out because he didn't like what his son said about my kids and how they played with him. My kids could hear this all taking place, as could my neighbors, but I kept my cool, waited for a few moments, then I took my revenge on the man. I answered him kindly and gently. I can tell he feels exhausted as a dad and there's obviously got to be a lot going on that would push a father to the point of that kind of reaction.

I answered him the way I would hope someone would speak to me if I was in the same situation as him. I didn't react to him or get fired up. He calmed down and I could tell that some part of him probably felt a little embarrassed for reacting like he did.

I was also glad that my kids had the opportunity to witness this. It fostered good discussion and turned into a very teachable moment in our home.

There is a proverb in the Bible that speaks to moments like this that I think would be wise for all leaders to commit to memory. It's something I think of as my favorite form of revenge, particularly because it really isn't vengeful at all.

In Proverbs 15:1 it says, *"A soft answer turns away wrath, but a harsh word stirs up anger."*

What a powerful and wise truth that is. If you're a leader, you have the opportunity to steer a situation in a better direction by how you respond. You can stir up anger when dealing with difficult people, or you can diffuse the situation and turn away wrath by answering gently when an irrational person needs to be calmed down.

I love doing that. I love watching the results. I love the fact that in addition to bringing peace to a difficult situation, it also seems to foster a healthy mindset within me. I don't leave those situations feeling like I have lost something or feeling like I'm a terrible person.

By responding in a healthy way to an unhealthy circumstance, I feel like I walk away feeling satisfied that I did the right thing and, for that matter, I feel like I'm responding in a way that Jesus modeled and He would approve of. That's important to me.

Let's be honest, there is someone who is going to put you to the test at some point, maybe today or maybe sometime soon. When that happens, don't be petty and immature just because they are. Rise up, keep your cool, and structure your revenge so that it isn't vengeful at all. Show them the kindness and maturity that they should have shown to you. Even if they never reciprocate it, you'll know that at least you responded like a wise leader when your leadership was put to the test.

Chapter 6

Your identity is not what you do

Who are you?

What do you most identify with in this world?

There are many aspects of leadership that feel mysterious to leaders, particularly during the early seasons of their leadership, but there is something that many leaders and people who live their lives in the public eye desperately need to understand (and hopefully they come to understand it sooner rather than later). It's the concept of "your identity" and I'll warn you at the start of this chapter that I believe the truest way to look at the concept of personal identity is from an eternal perspective as opposed to a momentary or situational perspective. I'll explain what I mean in a few moments.

And even if you aren't a particularly "spiritual" person, I hope you'll still give consideration with the concept I share in this chapter.

A moment ago, I asked you the question, "Who are you?" How do you answer that question? Or maybe better yet, if I asked the question by using your name, as in, "Who is _____?", how would you answer?

When I ask that question, I'm asking a question about your identity, but I don't usually get an answer that's related to an identity. The answers I get are usually related to an ability and there's a big difference between identity and ability.

In the vast majority of cases, when I ask someone that question, they'll usually say something like this, "Well, I'm a hard worker and a faithful husband. I never take a sick day. I study my craft thoroughly and I make intentional investments in myself. I like to laugh. I like warm weather and I don't eat seafood. I am a marathon runner and a 3-year participant in Tough Mudder. I am an engineer, a vice president in my company and a fan of the Philadelphia, Phillies."

That's a pretty thorough answer and even though I drew it out for effect, it's not very different from the kind of answers I get when I ask people that question. But does that response actually answer the question I asked? Does that response answer the question, "Who are you?"

Even though that answer was thorough, I would contend that it doesn't answer my question about identity. It's a good answer to a different question, but it doesn't answer the question "Who are you?"

The example answer I just gave you illustrates a mistake that all leaders are tempted to make, but the best leaders learn identify and correct. The answer my fictitious person gave was actually the answer to the questions, "What do you do?" and "What do you like?" It isn't an answer to the question, "Who are you?"

The truth is, there's a huge difference between who you are and what you do and leaders need to be extremely careful not to confuse the two.

Let me use myself as an example. Should my identity be wrapped up in the fact that I serve as the pastor of a local church? Could you see any danger in me possibly doing that? I will say that I do have a few colleagues who do seem to wrap their identity up in the fact that they are pastors or doctors or professors, but I would contend that that's a bad idea.

In my case, I already know that I won't always be the pastor of a local church. Someday I'll either retire, take a break or even sense a calling to serve in a different role. I have no idea. I can't predict that, I can only guess. I also know that someday, I'll die, so that pretty much guarantees that I won't always be pastoring a local church.

Wrapping my identity around something I do is a big mistake because what I do can quickly and easily change. My church might fire me when they discover that I'm a fan of professional wrestling or when they discover that there are way better pastors in this world they could hire. So if my identity is tied to my job, I'm setting myself up for a big fall at some point when some level of change inevitably comes to my day-to-day work experience.

Or take Michael Jordan for example. I used to love watching him play basketball. He was great on the court and was quickly recognized as one of the best, if not the best basketball player of all time. But what is Jordan doing now, other than sleeping on stacks of $1,000 dollar bills? He isn't playing basketball for the Bulls or the Wizards anymore, is he?

In fact, not long ago, I read an article that seemed to indicate that Jordan spends a fair amount of time longing for the days when he was on top of his game and that longing produces some level of sadness in his heart. What does this indicate to you? Do you suppose that he might be wrestling with the tension of basing his identity on his ability?

But what happens if your ability changes? What happens if your opportunities change? What happens if you're replaced by someone new? What happens if you develop an illness that limits what you can do? What happens if your industry becomes obsolete? You see where I'm going?

What I'm saying is that if something won't always be true of you, then your identity should not be tied to it. If it can change or be taken away or lost, then your identity should never be tied to it because in that case, you would be confusing your identity with an ability and our abilities are always fluctuating.

This can also be a big reason why some leaders struggle with criticism and find it difficult to process. If their identity is being tied to a temporary ability, then they won't know how to process a critique of their work. Instead of reflecting on how they might be able to improve or adjust their performance, they'll immediately get defensive or depressed because they'll interpret commentary on their effort or ability as a judgement on who they are as a person.

So what should we do as leaders and public figures to prevent this from happening? I think we need to start asking ourselves questions that are more eternally focused in nature. Please permit me to share some details of my core beliefs. Even if you come from a different perspective, I believe this will be beneficial.

For me, as a person of faith, the way I process this is to try to look at myself through the lens of God's eyes. Meaning, when He looks at me, what does He see? How would He answer the question of who am I? In His Word (the Bible) I'm told that through faith in Jesus, my identity is eternally tied to Christ. As God the Father sees God the Son, so too does He see me since I am looked at as being united to Christ. That means that when it's time for me to wrestle with the question, "Who are you?", the only way I can answer that question honestly is to acknowledge what will be true of me forever.

The Bible teaches that forever, I am a child of God. Forever, I am loved. Forever, I am forgiven. Forever, I am welcomed into His presence with joy because I am united by faith to Jesus Christ, the Son of God.

I find this very healthy and encouraging to dwell on personally and I hope you'll consider dwelling on this concept as well. Not long ago, I put a really brief book together on the subject that lists 100 aspects of our identity in Christ. The book is called, *"Your Identity in Christ - 100 powerful reminders of who you truly are in Jesus."* The book is so brief that you can probably read it through in 20 minutes, but the reminders are so helpful for me to realize and dwell upon when I'm tempted to forget who I really am in God's eyes.

If you're reading this book and not a person of faith, I probably just thoroughly weirded you out and I guess that's the risk you run when you read one of my books, but just the same, please remember that your identity and your abilities are not one and the same.

What you do is temporary.

Who you are is eternal.

Chapter 7

Taking action and gaining respect

Good leaders operate differently from the patterns employed by most people. There's actually a big difference that separates effective leaders from the rest of the crowd. Many people talk about their goals, but leaders take action.

What do I mean by taking action? Very simply, healthy leadership involves a combination of insight, decision making and then acting on what gets decided.

Let me give you an example of how I have seen this play out. How many times have you heard people say that someday, they intended to write a book? I would say that easily, I have heard dozens if not hundreds of people say that someday, they intend to do that. They intend to share their life story. They intend to share their experiences. They intend to write about insights they've gained, BUT, they never do it. They just talk about doing it.

Well, how hard is it to write a book? The truth is, it's not very difficult at all. At this point, I have published 13 books and I have several others in the works. By the time you read this, I hope to have published at least ten more. When you want to write a book, all you need to do is get an idea, outline what you want to write, read up on additional info. that you might want to include, then write the book.

You don't have to do it all in one day, but you do need to make progress on it. You don't even need to tell yourself that you're going to write a book if that sounds to large of a task. All you need to do is to write out a page of content and then do that 50 or 100 times more. Then, before you know it, you've written a book. You can pay someone else to edit it. You can pay someone else to create the cover and Amazon will let you publish it on their website for free.

But it's easier to talk about writing a book than it is to write one. It's easier to daydream than it is to do. And some people are really good at daydreaming and talking they they are at taking action. I would encourage you, if you're someone who is better at daydreaming and talking than taking action, that you seriously consider keeping your daydreams and ideas to yourself instead of sharing them with others. Why would I say that?

Well, if you're primarily a talker or a dreamer and not a doer, eventually, people will stop listening to you. You'll lose their trust. You'll damage your credibility and you'll inhibit your ability to get things done when you finally do get around to taking action.

I'll never forget a brief conversation I had with an older lady after a worship service that involved groups of people from about 20 different churches. She came up to talk to me afterward and told me which church she attended. I said, "Oh, I've heard of your church. In fact, I know your pastor. He's a nice guy. We grab lunch together sometimes."

She seemed to appreciate that and in the midst of our conversation, she started talking about a guitarist she had heard and enjoyed. I happened to mention that her pastor had also shared quite openly that he was practicing and learning to play guitar so that one day he could add that to the worship service at their church. I said this in a complimentary way, but she laughed at that comment and said, "Yeah, I'll believe it when I see it. Sounds like another empty promise from our pastor. He'll never actually do it."

Ouch. That was awkward. It turns out that he was more a dreamer than a doer and the longer he served in his church, the less they believed him when he spoke because he rarely seemed to follow up his words with action.

I don't know who to attribute this quote to, so if you know where this originated, please let me know, but somewhere along the way, someone once said, *"If you want people to respect you, always do exactly what you tell people you're going to do."* I think that's true. I think it's an issue of honesty, integrity and good leadership.

I also like to add an addendum to that quote. *"If you discover you can't do what you said you were going to do because circumstances changed or you no longer believe it would be a wise course of action, take the time to explain why you are no longer taking the action you originally intended to take."* People understand that circumstances change and they'll forgive you when you're upfront about a change of plans.

A historical leader that I personally have a lot of respect for is President Theodore Roosevelt. I reference him quite regularly and often think about some of the decisions he made and the actions he took. Teddy Roosevelt was a man of action and even people who didn't personally like him couldn't help but respect him because when he said he was going to do something, he did it. Yes, he was a dreamer and yes, he was a talker, but he followed up his dreams and his speeches with action and the United States and this world can still see the effects of what he did, even though he's been dead for nearly 100 years.

Just listen to some of the things he said about taking

action:

> "Far better it is to dare mighty things, to win glorious triumphs even though checkered by failure, than to rank with those poor spirits who neither enjoy nor suffer much because they live in that gray twilight that knows neither victory nor defeat."

> "It is not the critic who counts; not the man who points out how the strong man stumbled or where the doer of deeds could have done them better. The credit belongs to the man who is actually in the arena, whose face is marred by dust and sweat and blood; who strives valiantly; who errs and comes short again and again; who knows great enthusiasms, the great devotions; who spends himself in a worthy cause; who at the best, knows in the end the triumph of high achievement, and who, at the worst, if he fails, at least fails while daring greatly so that his place shall never be with those timid souls who neither know victory nor defeat."

During Roosevelt's life, he preserved great tracts of land, facilitated the building of the Panama Canal, wrote countless books, took fascinating and dangerous trips, organized a team of soldiers, volunteered for war service, brought organization and integrity to a corrupt police department, governed a state and led a nation. Admittedly, anyone who knew him or has studied him could testify that he didn't do any of these things perfectly, but that's not my point in sharing this. In fact, the unattainable desire for perfection usually puts the breaks on getting worthwhile things accomplished.

My point in bringing Teddy Roosevelt up as an example

was that he was the type of guy who didn't sit around talking or waiting for someone else to get something done. He saw a need, contemplated a solution and took the action he needed to take to get things done. He was a man of action, not a man of vain rhetoric.

So, if you've been entrusted with a role of leadership, make the most of it by being a person of action. Let it be that when others hear you speak, they grow confident that whatever you say, you're going to do your best to follow through with doing it. Be a person who excels at follow through. Take a moment to see a need, outline what needs to get done then take action to get it accomplished.

I think you'll begin to see that even if others don't always agree with the course of action you take, they will develop respect for you as a leader who doesn't just talk in vain platitudes and ideas, but as a leader who gets things done to the best of your ability for the good of those you have been called to lead.

Chapter 8

The greatest leaders are servants

There is a concept that is very difficult for many people to accept, but is highly embraced by the best leaders. It's a concept that most leaders would probably say has taken them a lifetime to gain a better grasp on. The concept I'm referring to is servanthood.

What it means to serve those you have been called to lead? I realize that servanthood probably sounds like the opposite of leadership, but I can assure you that cultivating a servants heart is actually an enhancement to your leadership.

By nature, what do most people perceive leadership to be like? Now, if you're a seasoned leader, you know this assumption is ridiculously false, but what is the illusion many people have about leadership? I think many people think of leaders as people who have the opportunity to boss others around, get their way and rarely have to lift a finger. And in thinking of themselves as leaders one day, while they may resent those who lead in a bossy way, I think some people actually daydream about leading in that very same way.

But is that what leadership is actually like? Do leaders who operate in a bossy or arrogant manner find themselves leading people for a significantly long time AND do they experience people thanking them for the impact of their leadership? Rarely, if ever.

Good leadership and arrogance aren't compatible. Good leadership and a dictatorial personality aren't compatible either. In fact, the most impactful and influential leaders are those who realize that their real job is to serve others and provide something of legitimate value to those they lead.

A great example of the concept of servant leadership is mentioned by Gary Inrig in his book, "A Call to Excellence." In that book, he tells the story of an event that occurred during the ministry of famous pastor and evangelist, D.L. Moody.

Moody was leading a conference at the time in Massachusetts and people came from great distances, even from other countries to hear him. Gary Inrig tells the rest of the story. In his book, he says it like this...

> *A large group of European pastors came to one of D. L. Moody's Northfield Bible Conferences in Massachusetts in the late 1800s. Following the European custom of the time, each guest put his shoes outside his room to be cleaned by the hall servants overnight. But of course this was America and there were no hall servants.*
>
> *Walking the dormitory halls that night, Moody saw the shoes and determined not to embarrass his brothers. He mentioned the need to some ministerial students who were there, but met with only silence or pious excuses. Moody returned to the dorm, gathered up the shoes, and, alone in his room, the world's only famous evangelist began to clean and polish the shoes. Only the unexpected arrival of a friend in the midst of the work revealed the secret.*
>
> *When the foreign visitors opened their doors the*

next morning, their shoes were shined. They never knew by whom. Moody told no one, but his friend told a few people, and during the rest of the conference, different men volunteered to shine the shoes in secret. Perhaps the episode is a vital insight into why God used D. L. Moody as He did. He was a man with a servant's heart and that was the basis of his true greatness. 1

I appreciate that story. I find it motivating and it does a good job of illustrating the kind of heart that a person of influence should cultivate. The heart of a servant.

But of course we naturally find ourselves resisting that kind of action because, to a degree, it seems a bit humiliating. I'm sure many people would look at an opportunity to serve others like that and consider it beneath their dignity to have to take the smelly shoes of those who travelled across the ocean to hear you preach and teach, and then shine those shoes without so much as a pat on the back for the effort.

We would much rather bark out orders to others to do our dirty work (and this world is filled with plenty of people who try to lead like that). But as we all can testify, that's not the kind of leadership this world needs nor is the kind of leadership that many of us find attractive or desirable.

Arrogant leadership doesn't invite loyalty and it doesn't produce lasting influence. As we discussed a few chapters back, leadership is influence. Whether or not you have a title is practically irrelevant. If you're influencing others, you're already leading them. But you can't influence those you repel and arrogance is a "people repellant."

Admittedly, servant leadership can be a confusing thing. It's sometimes confusing for those who try to practice it because it forces us to swallow our pride and serve when we'd much rather bark out orders and receive. But servant leadership can also be initially confusing to those on the receiving end, even if they can perceive a direct benefit to themselves from being served by their leaders. So it's possible that they may actually resist it until they come to understand it.

A great example of this can be seen in the New Testament book of John. In Chapter 13 of the book, we're given a glimpse of the servant heart of Jesus Christ as he humbly stooped to wash His disciples' feet. This is what the passage says...

> *Jesus knew that the Father had given him authority over everything and that he had come from God and would return to God. So he got up from the table, took off his robe, wrapped a towel around his waist, and poured water into a basin. Then he began to wash the disciples' feet, drying them with the towel he had around him.*
>
> *When Jesus came to Simon Peter, Peter said to him, "Lord, are you going to wash my feet?"*
>
> *Jesus replied, "You don't understand now what I am doing, but someday you will."*
>
> *"No," Peter protested, "you will never ever wash my feet!"*
>
> *Jesus replied, "Unless I wash you, you won't belong to me." (John 13:3-8, NLT)*

The truth is, real leadership isn't as glamorous as people like to think it is. When you peel the curtain back, you can see that leadership involves serving others. It may require you to place yourself in awkward circumstances. It may force you to get your hands dirty. It may require you to engage in actions that at one point you thought were beneath you. But the best leaders are those who show us what it's like to shun arrogance and are willing serve others, not for the fame of the one doing the serving, but for the benefit of the one being served.

Don't be afraid to get your hands dirty by serving someone today. Don't worry about doing things that are beneath you. The great leaders who preceded you weren't afraid to get their hands dirty. Their humility and selfless spirit attracts us to their example and you're very likely to find that as you actively practice servant leadership, your ability to lead others won't be diminished. It will actually be strengthened and enabled to grow.

Notes: 1. Gary Inrig, A Call to Excellence, (Victor Books, a division of SP Publ., Wheaton, Ill; 1985), p. 98

Chapter 9

Three words every leader needs to say

There are three brief words that all good leaders should admit to themselves and then actively communicate with their team. These words can be difficult at times to say, but every team needs to hear them. It's a simple series of three words and they are, *"I need you."*

As I have already mentioned, there are times when serving in leadership can be lonely. Many leaders confess to feeling lonely in their roles. There are many things that contribute to that feeling of loneliness, and one of the contributors can often be a leader's hesitancy to admit to himself that he needs help, which may then translate into a hesitancy on his part to communicate to his team that he needs help.

Leaders need to grow comfortable with saying three specific words, "I need you."

I was reminded of this fact while attending a training session a while back with John Maxwell. John Maxwell is widely recognized as the dominant voice on the subject of leadership in this era. I don't know how many books he has written, but there's quite a few, possibly more than 60. Many people look to him for advice, encouragement and inspiration as they seek to lead in their organizations.

At this season of life, we could presume that John has it made. He's sold millions of books, so he's financially set. He's respected by his peers and even invited by the heads of nations to come and train their national leadership. I have met people who seem to hang on his every word.

I appreciate his books, his leadership example and the investment that he makes in the lives of other leaders, but I was particularly impressed by three words he communicated to the men and women he was training alongside me. He looked at us and repeatedly said, *"I need you."*

That seems like a funny concept to be communicated from a man like him. In many respects, you wouldn't assume that he would sense a need for very many things in life. He's accomplished more than most people ever dream to do, yet with sincerity, he made sure that the leaders he was training heard him say how much he needed them.

That had an impact on me and it reminded me of something that I don't think I do enough of - something that I have been doing my best to be more intentional about ever since. I want the team of people that I have the privilege to work with to know just how much I need them.

In our church organization, there are many moving parts and since the launch of the church, we have created various Ministry Director positions to help oversee these departments of the church. We have directors who oversee; finances, hospitality, greeting, sound and technology, nursery care, children's and youth programs, communication, music, congregational care, administration, Summer programs and building care. I often say, and I truly mean this, that if there is anything that someone might appreciate about our church, it is being led by one of our Ministry Directors and their teams.

I need them. Our church needs them.

In the early days of our church, there was just a bare bones group of us who would wear just about every hat there was. I personally wore more hats than I prefer to count. That gets old after a while and as the church started to grow, it became nearly impossible to continue like that. Important needs were going unmet. I was getting burned out. The rest of our skeleton crew was as well. We needed help and by God's grace, He sent it in the form of our Ministry Directors.

We looked at our congregation, and considered the people that were part of it. We evaluated potential leaders based on their character, competency, compatibility and capacity, then asked people if they would be willing to serve in specific roles that fit with their gifts and their passions. Some said "yes", others said "no", but we began building our team with quality people who are awesome at what they do. Under their leadership, our young church continues to make progress and it grows healthier by the month.

I need them. Our church needs them. They need to hear me say, from time to time that I am aware of my need for them. I need to hear myself say it as well. Leadership would be unbearably lonely without them.

In your organization, there are people who surround you and help you do your job. You know that they are an asset to your organization and if they are quality people who meet the 4C's of character, competency, compatibility and capacity, they are contributing to the health of your organization. They are are also helping you bear the burden of leadership and investing their time by helping you implement your vision. Your vision would go nowhere without their help implementing and refining it. You may have good ideas, but in many respects, they are the people who help make those ideas come to life.

They need to hear you say, in very intentional ways, *"I*

need you."

Don't be afraid to communicate that. If up to this point, you have tried to give off the impression of being self-sufficient, please give that a rest. You're just making things harder for yourself by doing that. Conveying an attitude of self-sufficiency is a great way to chase the help you really need away. It's a great way to foster loneliness in leadership. It's a great way to burn yourself out by trying to live out a fallacy.

This isn't to say that you don't play an important role. You definitely do. But let's make this a two way street. You know that there are certain traits and abilities that you bring to the table that others need. You feel appreciated and motivated when others remind you of the value you bring to the table. Why not share the love a little more? It will benefit you, your team and your organization if you become intentional about letting the people who surround you and support your leadership know that you truly need them. Swallow your pride and bless them by saying it.

"I need you."

Chapter 10

Will you run or will you grow?

How do you respond to persistent challenges. I'm sure that over the course of your leadership, you have experienced protracted seasons of challenge and adversity. When that takes place, there are different ways we can handle it. One option is to turn tail and move on. The other option is to dig deep and grow.

If you're a leader, there are going to be times in the leading of your organization when things are going to feel like they're running very smoothly. Ideas are being implemented well. The people you serve are going to seem happy. Your team is going to feel motivated. Finances are going to be at a healthy state. It's all going to seem awesome.

Then, there are going to be seasons that present legitimate challenges. Your team may be grumbling. The people you're trying to serve are going to seem unhappy. Finances might be down and you'll be scratching your head as to what to do to get everything up and running again.

What do you do when you experience seasons like that? I will confess that I'm not a big fan of those seasons. I would much rather have everything moving along without any glitches, but that's not the reality of the ebb and flow of most any organization. Sometimes you're up, sometimes you're not. Sometimes everything is working great. Other times, you're struggling.

And making it even worse, sometimes the seasons when you're struggling feel like they're dragging on for an unreasonable amount of time. It feels like they just aren't going to end.

What do you do when you go through seasons like this? I can tell you what I see plenty of people do. They quit. They look at their difficult circumstances, start casting blame on themselves, internalize the criticism and critique they receive, start feeling terrible about themselves, and then they give up. They tap out and walk away. Their motivation for continuing the work that they began starts to dwindle and they remove themselves from the equation all together.

Now, let me say that there certainly can be a time when it's appropriate to move on. I'm not going to imply that every situation of leadership change is wrong or unhealthy, but I do want to say that more often than necessary, leaders throw the towel in too soon.

As a pastor, I have come to know quite a few pastors over the past 20 years or so and I'm friends with one man who seems to live someplace new every time I see him. He became a pastor right after college and he's a grandfather now. Most of the time, he seems to last right around 3 years when he moves to a new area. He's a delightful man and someone I very much appreciate, but he is highly adverse to conflict. Whenever he experiences conflict that lasts longer than the basic duration, he leaves. He runs away from it, and I would contend that his pattern of doing that has inhibited his growth as a leader. He's a great friend, but unfortunately, he isn't a strong leader.

Thankfully, there is another option we can consider when we're experiencing prolonged seasons of adversity. We don't always have to run. Sometimes, the best bet for everyone around is that we stay put, embrace the challenge, and choose to grow.

When I was a kid, I was fascinated with exercise. I was convinced that when I grew up, I was going to have huge muscles. (I'm still waiting on that...). I used to lift weights as a 10 and 11-year-old regularly. It hurt, but it made my muscles grow. I can even remember standing up in front of my 6th grade class and showing them how I could make my biceps move. My teacher thought that was hilarious. I wasn't sure what she thought was so funny.

Well, as much as I wish I was more fit and consistent with exercise as an adult, I do have an idea of how to facilitate the growth of muscles. For a muscle to grow, we all know that it needs to be used. It needs to be broken down by being regularly brought to its breaking point through exercise. And when this is consistently applied over time, the muscle grows strong.

Our experiences can have the same kind of effect on our growth as a leader. Our leadership capacity and our leadership wisdom both seem to grow when they're stretched or put under some level of pressure. We atrophy when we're just standing still, but prolonged seasons of challenge can really be a gift in disguise. They can turn out to be fantastic tools to help facilitate our growth in leadership.

When I look back over the past 20 years, I can think of seasons that weren't very pleasant. I can think of challenges I have faced and discouragements that were hard not to internalize and take very personally. But I can also testify that when I stuck it out and didn't run from those experiences, they were used in my life much like the gift of exercise. They helped me grow. They bolstered my confidence and they helped make me more fit for different challenges that I would need to face at later seasons of life and leadership.

And here's the other piece of good news. Every challenge that I have faced as a leader eventually came to an end. Challenges and trials are seasonal. They come and they go. We can lie to ourselves in the midst of them and tell ourselves that they're permanent in nature, but when we look back at what we've already been through, we can all see that what we've experienced in the past eventually came to an end - even the worst situations and circumstances.

So, if you're going through a prolonged season of adversity right now, you can do a couple things. You can decide it's time to move on, (and if you do make that decision, I hope you're correct and that you're not just becoming adept at avoiding conflict.) But the other option is that you can decide to embrace the challenge that has been placed before you. Don't internalize the words of your critics. Don't be overly harsh on yourself either. Just accept the fact that this season isn't as easy as previous seasons, but by design, it has the capacity to help you grow like easier seasons never could.

And if you embrace this season of adversity, get ready to grow stronger in determination, stronger in grit, stronger in patience, stronger in faith, and stronger in wisdom. You can choose to run if you want, but what I really hope you'll choose to do is grow.

Chapter 11

Why do good leaders mentor others?

Throughout the course of your life, who has invested their time in you?

Who are you investing your time in?

Good leaders make a point to invest their time in people with potential. They mentor others and they usually do this because they are conscious of the ways their life and leadership was developed and strengthened by those who mentored them.

I don't know if the word mentorship gets your attention or if it seems like something that isn't high on your scale of interest, but I'm going to do my best in this chapter to try to convince you that it's important.

Mentorship (or mentoring) is the process of bringing someone with less knowledge or experience into your circle of operation with the goal of helping them grow as a leader in whatever field you serve in. It involves offering your counsel, but it also involves asking the right questions to help pull out information from the person you're coaching or mentoring that they may already know, but may not be thinking about in the moment.

Mentorship takes time, it takes creativity and it may take an added dose of patience, but there are many mutual benefits to mentoring that I think make it a worthy activity to engage in.

If you're a leader, odds are, there was someone or possibly several people who took time to mentor you. The first kind of mentors that probably come to our mind are people we worked directly with who taught us how to accomplish various aspects of our job. Very likely they modeled what we were to do then they observed us trying to do it. In addition to that, they probably took time to explain to us important facets of our roles that we may not have understood, and they patiently coached us toward becoming skilled at what we do. We wouldn't be the kind of leaders we are without their help. They were a vital link in the chain to help us get where we are.

I think there are other kinds of mentors many of us are very likely to have experienced as well. I would consider some of the professors I studied under as mentors to a certain degree. I would also put authors and other teachers that I have never personally met in the category of "mentors of influence" because of the influence and impact their teaching has had on my life.

In many ways, we have all benefitted from teachers and mentors who have taken the time to intentionally invest in our growth. In the same way, I think that the best leaders are also people who take time to mentor others out of appreciation for those who poured into their own lives.

But there is an element to mentoring that I also think takes some discernment. There are people that we should be investing in in a mentoring kind of relationship and there are those who I think we shouldn't take the time to mentor, or at least I can say that I wouldn't choose to mentor them. Let me give you a few examples.

At present, there are several people in my life who

consider me either their leadership coach or their mentor. In fact, I just received a text the other day from a friend who reminded me that he considers me his mentor. At this point, I consider him more of a peer and a friend, but I was encouraged to think that that's how he still views me.

With each of these people, I have come alongside them and sought to do my best to pass on wisdom, counsel and the understanding that comes from my personal experiences. Each of them have shown themselves to be doers, not just talkers. They are people of character who are doing their best to serve others. They don't just sit around and wait for life to happen to them. Rather, they are agents of change who are eager to grow and they want to lead those who look to them for leadership to the best of their ability.

They are teachable and I appreciate the fact that they trust my counsel. They act on what we talk about and the chain reaction of their willingness to be coached translates into excellent work and great leadership in their organizations. They are young leaders who are doing their best to serve others well and I'm happy to invest my time, energy and thought into each of them.

But then there are others who I resist entering into a coaching or mentoring kind of relationship with. Earlier in this book, I mentioned that there are people in this world who are all talk and no action. This shows up in their work, their leadership, their self-discipline and their personal ambition. They dream, but they rarely do. And interestingly, they also tend to have no qualms about using up or even wasting the time of those who are gullible enough to give it to them.

I have been one of those gullible people at times, and I learned to regret it... the hard way.

I try my best to be kind with others. I'm far from perfect in this area, but I definitely try. Several years ago, I encountered a man who was not much younger than me and he asked if I'd be willing to get together with him, mentor him and chat about life and some other ideas he had. He had visions of being a great leader and he wanted me to work with him to help him in that area. I told him I was willing to do so, but in retrospect, I should have investigated the situation more closely.

I'll save you most of the details, but I soon learned that he was all talk. He didn't follow through on most things including areas of self-discipline. It never bothered his conscience to use up as much of my time as he could. He would show up at my office regularly, unannounced, with new emergencies all the time. When he wasn't showing up, he would call me. When he wasn't calling me, he would message me on Facebook. Dealing with him was taking so much time, it was wearing me down.

I finally had to tell him that this had to stop. I should have said it sooner, but I was trying to be nice. He didn't understand boundaries and the kind of help he needed was beyond what I personally had the time to give him. I should have investigated a little further at the start before agreeing to begin mentoring him. He and I were not a good fit for that kind of relationship.

So, getting back to a more positive line of thought, why should mentorship be something that we as leaders invest our time in? Let me suggest six reasons.

1. It is intrinsically right and is how life is designed to work. The older mentor the younger. The more experienced mentor the less experienced.

2. It has the potential to benefit your mission as an organization by creating a stream of the next rung of capable leaders who can serve in ways that you serve,

with some of your unique leadership DNA present in the process.

3. It is beneficial for those being mentored. It's healthy to do things that aren't solely for our personal benefit. It produces a healthy sense of "others-centered thinking."

4. It will help keep you healthy and sharp as a leader by creating healthy outlets through which your insight can flow and give you a place where you can refine your teaching and communicating skills.

5. It will keep you from becoming a selfish leader.

6. It will often produce a source of encouragement to you. Many leaders share that some of their greatest joys in their field of service have come through observing the success of those they have mentored.

Speaking of encouragement, I can tell you that there are several people I have mentored who have reached out to me this year to tell me that they appreciated something that I modeled or explained for them in the past. Interestingly, and I believe God's fingerprints were all over this, they seemed to reach out to me during seasons when I was feeling a little down or discouraged. I thought that was fascinating, but I can tell you from those experiences, the fact that I mentored these individuals was something that has had a boomerang effect in that it has come back to me in words of encouragement and appreciation, sometimes years after the fact.

So, what do you think? Is mentoring others worth your time and effort? Is it something that you would consider doing for the greater good of your organization, for the development of a new generation of leaders and for the sake of keeping your leadership sharp and your heart soft? I think it's worth it and I hope you'll consider carving out time to do it if you interact with people who have great potential that would benefit from your wisdom and experience.

Chapter 12

What is your level of teachability?

Over the course of my life as I have interacted many different people who were serving in roles of leadership, I have learned that there is a personality trait that I believe is a major indicator of whether or not a person will actually become a successful leader in their field or organization. It's the issue of teachability and I have an "anecdotal case study" that I want to tell you about. It's something that I have had the opportunity to observe over the past 20 years and it directly relates to the teachability or lack of teachability of one particular leader and how that played out in his life. I share about that case study in a moment.

Teachability in a leader's life is basically his willingness and eagerness to learn or be taught new things. Some leaders are quite teachable and some are not. In my experience, the best leaders are teachable and the worst leaders are not. Great leaders want to grow and learn, and bad leaders convince themselves that they already know everything they need to know and for that reason, they stagnate and operate in a state of willful ignorance which ends up hurting them, hurting their team and hurting the people they are trying to serve.

I once heard a story about Abraham Lincoln that I

thought was very interesting. I have a great book in my office about the way Lincoln led. The book is called "Lincoln on Leadership" by Donald T. Phillips and it's an excellent read that I would highly recommend.

The majority of Lincoln's time in office was spent with the nation at war. It was a difficult time in American history, to say the least, and Lincoln had been thrust, by virtue of being elected president, into the role of Commander and Chief of the Armed Forces. No sweat, right? Hardly.

I can just imagine what that must have been like. Every day, people relied on Lincoln to make decisions and appoint the right leaders to carry out those decisions. Every day Lincoln was faced with making decisions regarding the war that had a direct impact on whether people lived or people died. And he saw plenty of this carnage first hand and lived with the reality that in some respects, the war was taking place not far from the front door of the White House.

What would you do if you were put in that kind of position? Do you think you would be able to sleep much at night or do you think that the weight of the kind of decisions you had to make would keep you up at night? You know what Lincoln did in the midst of this dark season of American history? He studied.

Listen to this tidbit from the Smithsonian about Lincoln's leadership as Commander in Chief...

> *He read and absorbed works on military history and strategy; he observed the successes and failures of his own and the enemy's military commanders and drew apt conclusions; he made mistakes and learned from them; he applied his large quotient of common sense to slice through the obfuscations and excuses of military subordinates. By 1862 his grasp of strategy and*

operations was firm enough almost to justify the overstated but not entirely wrong conclusion of historian T. Harry Williams: "Lincoln stands out as a great war president, probably the greatest in our history, and a great natural strategist, a better one than any of his generals." **1**

    Lincoln read, studied, observed and learned. He was a life-long learner. Throughout his life, he was a man who was motivated to learn what he needed to know so that he could do what he needed to do as well as he could possibly do it. This applied to his time as a lawyer and it also applied to his time as president. 150 years after the fact, many people still consider him one of the best, if not the best president the United States ever had.

    Good leaders learn. They're always expanding their understanding. They don't want to stagnate or dry out. They're invested in their personal growth and maturity and they intentionally invest in getting the information, education and training they need so they can serve and lead effectively. They are curious and they are invested in their development as a leader.

    But then you have those who fall in the other category - leaders who feel like they already know everything they need to know so at this point, they have lazily given up on themselves. I don't admire leadership that falls into this category. Leaders that stop being intentional about their growth are leaders that should probably turn in the keys to the building and move along to the golf course because they're more likely than not to end up damaging the people they're supposed to be leading because they prefer to live life dwelling in a "less informed cubicle."

    I mentioned earlier that I had the opportunity to witness this play out first hand. Over the past 20 years, I have watched one particular man, out of his own insecurities and hard-headedness, resist counsel and advice that challenged what he thought he knew and challenged his personal preferences in leadership.

20 years ago, I went with a group of pastors and other church leaders through training that was geared toward creating a healthy culture of leadership, growth and involvement among the members of the individual churches we led. The training was helpful and insightful. It helped facilitate what it said it would, when put into practice.

One man who was invited to attend chose not to. When he was asked why, he said, "I have been to so many of these things that at this point, I could teach them myself." I directly heard him make that statement, but I also wondered why, if he was so well-informed, he wasn't implementing these concepts in his church.

For the next 20 years, I watched him bounce around, irritating people with his arrogance and lack of teachability. I also watched as the ministries he was responsible to lead suffered and declined under his leadership. This man wasn't teachable. He was in a position of leadership, but he chose to become like a pond that had run dry. He stopped investing in his growth and understanding, and the people who served under his leadership and the organizations he led suffered as a result.

So, how can we avoid this kind of outcome in our own lives? How can we remain teachable and where can we go to make intentional investments in our understanding, education and training as leaders?

Thankfully, this question is easier to answer than ever. We're surrounded, even bombarded with opportunities to learn and grow. To narrow this down, however, I'll share several sources of information and education that have been helpful to me.

Here's my list:
1. Podcasts
2. Webinars / YouTube
3. Blogs
4. Conferences
5. Paid training
6. Books
7. Roundtables with other leaders (I like surrounding myself with other leaders).
8. Formalized education and workshops offered by universities
9. Ted talks (to a degree, but admittedly some are more inspiring than they are practical)

That's some of what I have found helpful to me. I always seem to leave with new information or ideas when I carve time out to invest in my growth as a leader and when I choose to remain teachable instead of unreachable and ignorant.

Even some of the boring conferences and seminars I have attended have been helpful. If I'm not getting much out of the session, I am still thankful for the opportunity to sit still for a minute and potentially be prompted by the discussion to think deeper about my own situation and leadership role.

All that to say, remaining teachable and curious are key to your success as a leader. This gets harder as we grow older, but don't give up on investing in your understanding. Don't close yourself off from new ideas, insights or updated approaches. You'll stay fresher as a leader and you'll put yourself in a position where you can better serve the people you're trying to lead.

Note: 1 http://www.smithsonianmag.com/history/lincoln-as-commander-in-chief-131322819/#x6KvHv6HgXoe7fYY.99

Chapter 13

Eight principles for dealing with unrealistic expectations

"Expectations" are a very real thing. If you're a leader, I'm sure you've come to realize that the people you lead, serve and work with have varying expectations of you, many of which are so lofty, they are impossible for you to meet. So what do you do? How do you balance doing what you need to do and meeting the sometimes unattainable expectations of those you lead?

The expectations those under your leadership have of you are likely to be high, maybe even unrealistically high. And in addition to that, the high expectations they have of you probably differs from person to person based on what they feel they need most from you.

How do you react to that reality? Do you ever grow frustrated with it? It can seem rather impossible when you try to meet the many expectations others have for you in your role because the expectations can be so different and they may be quite different from what you understand your role to be in the first place.

In your mind, you probably have a well-defined vision for what your role is. There are things that you clearly see as your role and things that you don't believe are functions of the role you serve in. Others may disagree and when it comes down to it, they will primarily view your role through the lens of how it impacts them, with little to no thought for what it's like to be in your shoes or do what you do.

Even more impossible are contexts where people not only cast unrealistic expectations on you, but they also expect you to read their mind and draw correct conclusions about what they're thinking you should be doing.

Let me give you an example from my experience as a leader in a pastoral role. Regardless of your specific role of leadership, I think you will find that some of these experiences are common to just about all leaders.

Different people have different expectations for leaders who serve in the role of pastor. There are people who expect pastors to wear any one of the following hats:

- Theologian
- Visionary
- Communicator
- Executive
- Nurturer
- Counselor
- Officiant, etc.

I look at that list and I realize a few things about myself. I am strong in several of those areas and weak in others. I consider myself a capable communicator, but I also consider myself a poor nurturer. I naturally gravitate toward teaching, but I don't tend to excel at needs-based care. I wish I was good at both, but I'm not and from time to time, I'm reminded of that. It makes me feel guilty sometimes because I wish I was good at everything everyone wants me to be good at, but that's not realistic so it's not healthy for me to internalize those kinds of expectations of myself.

Making that even trickier for pastors and other leaders is that some people aren't very clear about their expectations of you or clear about what they may need from you. They leave you guessing. They play a game where they sit and wait for you to read their mind until they become upset when they realize that you're not willing to play that game with them.

I'll never forget an experience I had about 10 years ago. I was confronted by a woman who regularly attended services at our church, but wasn't involved in the rest of what took place during the week, so I never got to know her very well. She was angry with me and confronted me because I didn't attend the viewing or the funeral services for a member of her extended family that had passed away. She expected that her pastor would do that. She saw my role through a ceremonial kind of lens and she was let down when I didn't do what she expected me to do.

There were a couple problems with her expectations. First of all, I didn't know the extended family member. Second, I didn't know they died. Third, I didn't know about their viewing or funeral. And fourth, I didn't know she wanted me to come to these events. If she made any of this known to me, I would have been happy to be there for her. But I didn't know about any of it until she lashed out on me. And of course, she made sure to do it right after a worship service while I was greeting people in the back of the church. Lovely.

I listened to her politely and did my best to avoid getting defensive, but when it was appropriate to do so, I responded and said, "I would have been happy to be there if I knew about it." At that, she continued her awkward confrontation, so I replied a little more directly and said, "I'm good at a few things, but one thing I'm terrible at is reading people's minds. I will be happy to be present at future events, but I will need you to tell me about them first." And I left it at that.

Interestingly, I noticed after that that she seemed to act more reasonable toward me in future weeks and months. I'm guessing that maybe she gained a glimpse into my perspective or maybe she realized that she was responding in a weakened moment of grief when she yelled at me. Either way, our relationship and our ability to interact with each other seemed to improve and grow over time.

It's complicated though when people want you to read their mind. It's impossible and it guarantees that you will not meet their expectations of you or your performance as a leader.

Let me share eight quick principles that I think are valuable to keep in mind when dealing with the expectations of others and how they view your role of leadership.

1. Everyone has a different expectation of you.

2. You won't be able to meet every expectation people have of you.

3. You will eventually let someone down, and that's ok.

4. Letting people down isn't a commentary on your value and strengths.

5. More likely, it is a commentary on them and their desires.

6. You're good at some things, but not all things. No one is and that's totally fine.

7. Do what you do well.

8. Accept that it is impossible to be or do everything others may expect you to be or do.

At some point, I'm sure you've been tested with this same kind of experience. I'm tested by this on a weekly basis and if I let it, it would drive me insane. It certainly has produced some discouraging moments for me over the years, so I find it quite helpful to realize that I don't have to be perfect. I won't be able to meet everyone's expectations of me and that's ok. As much as I don't want to, I will at times let people down. That doesn't mean I'm a bad person or a bad leader. All it often means is that their expectations of me and my expectations don't match up. And I'm learning to accept that I need to stay focused on what I'm supposed to do and not worry about meeting expectations that are unfair or unrealistic.

I hope you're also coming to accept the same thing regarding yourself and your role.

Chapter 14

How to overcome your fear of public speaking

Do you enjoy speaking in front of groups?

I don't know how many times in your life you've been asked to give a speech, but I'm assuming that if you're in leadership or if you're aspiring to be more highly involved in leadership, public speaking is something that you're going to have to get used to doing. But the interesting thing about public speaking is that it terrifies most people. It truly freaks people out and maybe you would say that's true of you as well.

If you're terrified of public speaking, what can you do about that? How can you overcome your fear of speaking in front of large or even small groups? In this coming paragraphs, I'm going to share with you what works well for me. I'm certain it will be helpful to you as well.

You may have heard about this already, but I remember reading the results of a Reader's Digest survey that was taken years ago where they interviewed a large group of people and asked them to rank the things that caused them the most fear. Surprisingly the second most common fear was "death." And the number one fear of the group they surveyed was "public speaking." That means that more people were afraid of speaking in public than dying.

What do you think about public speaking? Can you remember the first time you were asked to speak in front of a group? I'm guessing that many of us had to do that in grade school or high school and I don't remember finding that too intimidating as a child because half the time, I would just use those moments to try to make my friends or the teacher laugh. It was a familiar and comfortable setting so it felt less intimidating to me.

But as I got older, I was asked to speak in a new context. I remember the leadership of the church I grew up in asking me to speak or read Scripture in front of the congregation right around the time I was 15. That was not a context where I could just goof around and while I said "yes," I was definitely intimidated by it.

I remember how sick my stomach would feel on Sunday mornings while I waited for the pastor to call me forward to read. I felt nauseas. I felt sweaty and I felt shaky. It was almost like the kind of feeling you get when your blood sugar drops too low.

Then I would stand in front of the church, read a Scripture passage and my voice would noticeably shake the entire time I was doing it. I remember asking my sister once, "How'd it go?" And she said, "You seemed extremely nervous up there, but I'm sure the church will forgive you. They like you enough." Some comfort that was.

In time, I started speaking more and more. I spoke to church groups and college groups. I taught and led the staff at our Summer Camp. I guest spoke wherever I was invited and while I was growing more skilled at public speaking, I still struggled with the fear of doing it and I know that fear took something away from the presentation.

Then I became a pastor and the job of a pastor involves

speaking all the time. You're constantly in front of groups, preaching and teaching. I can remember one Sunday very early in my ministry when I basically ran out of something to say after just a few minutes of speaking, so I awkwardly ended the service. I also remember my first moments as a pastor in a new church when I stood in the pulpit and then clumsily watched my Bible fall to the ground because I didn't set it on the pulpit the right way (again, because I was nervous).

Now at this season of my life, I also find myself speaking for retreats, conferences and organizations as well. Just a few weeks ago, I was speaking in front of 600 students at the university I studied at and this past Sunday, I guest spoke to a church of several hundred people.

And in the process of doing this over the course of my adult life, I have noticed something. For most of the years that I have been speaking, I have wrestled with feelings of fear and nervousness leading up to the event and even during the event, but that's been greatly diminished once I learned a powerful secret and I want to share that secret with you. This secret might not cure all nervousness or jitters, but it can dramatically reduce your fear of public speaking.

And the secret is this..... Focus on providing something of value for your audience and stop obsessing on how your audience will think of you. Focus on communicating something helpful. Don't obsessively focus on how you look while doing it.

Think about it for just a second. What are we most terrified about when we're speaking to a group? We're worried about getting up in front of a group and making a fool of ourselves. We're worried about how we're going to look and we're worried about what people are going to think about us afterward.

But what would it be like if we could take that fear off

the table? What if we used our energy to provide something valuable and helpful for those who are taking time to listen to us instead of using that energy to worry about how we're going to look during and after we speak?

I know for me this has made a huge difference. It helps me take the focus off of myself and it puts the focus on how I can best serve the people I'm trying to help. It keeps me focused on my content and the goal of what I'm trying to communicate and prevents me from stressing about what people are going to think about me afterward.

At one point, whether I fully admitted it to myself or not, I think my goal after speaking was that someone would compliment me. But now I'm speaking from a different approach. Today, my goal is that the people I'm speaking to would be helped. Helped to learn something new. Helped to see something from a more complete perspective. Encouraged. Inspired. Informed. Convicted. Challenged. I want to help those I'm speaking to, to learn something new or grow in what they've learned.

Once that became my focus, I began judging the success of a speech through a different metric. "How will this make me look?" was a metric that produced fear. "How will this help those I'm speaking to?" is a metric that has produced a healthier mindset because I'm taking the focus off of me and my benefit, and I'm choosing instead to focus on others and how I can bring something of benefit to them.

I'm convinced that if you can transition your focus from dwelling on how you're perceived to how other's are helped, you'll also begin to notice your fear of public speaking diminishing.

In addition to that, let me give you a few additional tips that might help you if you're asked to speak to a group. These aren't in any particular order.

1. Read, research and know what you're talking about.

2. Write out your speech like a manuscript and read it many times.

3. Read it right before you go to bed the night before the speech.

4. Don't fear sharing your personality or unique perspective. It's more interesting.

5. Make use of personal stories and experiences if they would be helpful.

6. Take one minute to introduce yourself and build rapport at the beginning.

7. Prepare your speech with a clear understanding of who you're speaking to.

8. Thank them for inviting you.

Public speaking is like many other skills. The only way to really get good at it is to do it regularly and experience can certainly help diminish fear. But even before you have years of experience under your belt, you can greatly reduce your fear if you start taking your focus off of what people might think about you and shift your focus toward how you can serve and provide something of value to those you're speaking to.

Chapter 15

How to not be a failure (even if you fail)

Leaders dream about doing "big" things, but there's a lingering fear that can get in the way of their pursuits. It's a fear that we've alluded to in a previous chapter, and it's a fear that will come up regularly in my conversations with other leaders. What is this fear that I'm alluding to?

The fear that I'm speaking about is the fear of failure. Is this something you wrestle with? Does it keep you from attempting big things? I imagine that the fear of failure is also something that keeps some people from ever sticking their neck out in leadership in the first place.

Let me say this right at the outset; You will never be able to grow in leadership to the level you should if you live in constant fear of failure. Failure is a reality. Failure is painful. Failure is inconvenient, but it isn't the enemy. Failure is an excellent teacher. Failure does a great job is contributing to our level of wisdom. Failure is helpful in rooting out various things that shouldn't be part of our lives to begin with.

I believe that good leaders learn to confront failure, instead of running from it. Good leaders don't let their failures turn into self-loathing or or their dominant internal commentary about their value as a person.

Every good leader has a series of failures they can point to and I would contend that you can't become a strong leader until you have a series of meaningful failures along the way.

The fact that you've experienced failure at different times of your life is most likely good evidence that you've been willing to attempt something big - something that others weren't quite as willing to try.

I think sometimes we imagine leadership, or entrepreneurship as if it goes along a line that's always pointing up, but that's not how it goes at all. It zig zags back and forth, up and down. You experience successes that keep you encouraged and motivated. Then they're followed up by setbacks or defeats. What do you do when that happens?

When we experience setbacks, we can give up, internalize our defeats, beat ourselves up and start making unhelpful comments about our character and our value OR we can call the setback what it is (a corrective learning experience), express thankfulness for this opportunity for growth, laugh about it a little, and press on.

I get bored with fantasy movies, but I can watch a good biography any day and I love watching biographies of leaders, particularly biographies of presidents and business entrepreneurs.

If you ever get the chance to watch the series, "The Men Who Built America", definitely check it out. It profiles the lives of Cornelius Vanderbilt, John D. Rockefeller, Andrew Carnegie, J.P. Morgan and Henry Ford and it also mentions a few other leaders and entrepreneurs. Some people watch that and their take away seems to be that these men were merely ruthless capitalists who didn't care about people. I don't think that's accurate. It's too simplistic and one dimensional to say that. I look at that documentary and see men who knew how to look for opportunity in the midst of failure.

The attempted very big things - projects that we take for granted every day, but things that were huge. These men made a direct impact on our system of finance, home heating, shipping, personal transportation, construction and the convenience of living in an electrified society. If they let their failures (and they all experienced big ones), prevent them from attempting big things, we wouldn't enjoy many of the major conveniences of modern life that we take for granted.

If you're a leader, there has to be some part of you that can laugh a little at your failures. So what if things didn't work out just right. So what if you made a mistake while trying to do something big. So what if you ended up with a little egg on your face here and there. You're doing what other people won't do because you're that rare person who dares to lead. Most people won't lead because they're afraid they'll fail. You're willing to lead because you view failure as a useful teacher that actually helps you become an even better leader.

Do me a favor and ask yourself right now, "What fears are currently holding me back from doing big things?" I'm guessing those fears might fall into one of the following categories.

1. How will this impact me financially?

2. How will this impact my family's comfort?

3. What will the people I care about think about me if this doesn't work?

4. What will I think about me if this doesn't work?

Earlier in this book, I shared a little about the trajectory of my leadership journey. Some aspects of my journey went well and according to a predictable plan. Other aspects were very difficult and included some royal failures. But when I start dwelling on my own failures, I like to remind myself of a couple things.

1. There was no guarantee that I wouldn't fail when I took on the leadership of the Pocono Mountain Bible Conference during a dark season in its history. It was so close to closing and in fact, some people were rooting for my failure, but thankfully, by God's grace, it didn't fail. If I was primarily governed by a fear of failure, I never would have accepted the risk of leading that organization and it could have closed back in 2003.

2. There was no guarantee that I wouldn't fail when I moved my family to Langhorne to attempt to plant our church. The previous church that met in the building was down to a few people (6 to 10 on a good Sunday) and about to shut down, but, having been bolstered by previous experiences, we took the risk and didn't let the fear of failure prevent us from doing what we were called to do. I didn't know if it would work, but I didn't want the fear of personal failure to prevent me from doing something that stretched my faith and perseverance.

What do you believe you're supposed to be doing during this season of your life? What's keeping you from sticking your neck out to do it? I'm not asking you to do something foolish or to attempt something major without the backing of solid counsel, but I do want to encourage you not to spend the brief decades you have on this planet consumed with an unhealthy level of the fear of failure. Be the leader you've been called to be and face that fear.

You might fail or you might not. But like I've said

before, I don't consider a man a failure if he tries and doesn't succeed. True failure, in my mind, is spending your entire life sitting on your hands because you're more concerned with how you might look to others than you are about getting something valuable accomplished for the good of others. Don't fear failure. Fear complacency.

Chapter 16

Keys to improving your personal finances

What do you think about money? Is money something good? Is it something evil? Is it neither?

I don't think money is good or evil. Money is like a table. It can be used for good purposes or bad purposes. A delicious meal can be served on a table or the legs can be broken off and used to beat someone senseless. Money has a similar function. It comes down to our personal motivations and whether we consider money to be a tool that has been entrusted to our stewardship by God or a if we live our lives as if money is our god.

I believe that leaders should exercise wisdom and caution when it comes to handling financial resources that are entrusted to them and that starts with their personal finances. This is a matter of practice that I believe is key for leaders to grasp and live out. We need to employ financial wisdom, not just in the organizations we lead (although that's vital), but also in our personal lives.

I'll be honest, I have not always been someone who managed my finances wisely so I'll share a few of the mistakes I've made and what I've learned from those mistakes. I'm also going to take the liberty to offer a few suggestions that I hope will be helpful if you're trying to improve your financial picture and employ more wisdom in how you manage your finances.

I believe that the way we manage our finances gives us a glimpse into our minds, our priorities, our disciplines and our heart desires. If those areas are in a state of disorientation, that disorientation will also very likely show up in our financial picture.

For just a moment, let's be students of our culture. I realize that some of you who are reading these pages come from places in this world that I have never been, so I can't truly say I know how this may operate in your culture. But here in the United States, we tend to be big on consumption and debt. Our culture emphasizes both and if we're not careful, we can buy into that mindset and then end up in very difficult financial circumstances.

This becomes very apparent every year in the United States as we approach the Christmas shopping season. People in our culture spend the last few weeks and months of every year overspending, over-consuming and accumulating harmful debt. Many people in our culture will spend more in the month of December than at any other time during the year. And in the end, it's all going to be for nothing. The majority of what's purchased won't get used. It will just sit around and take up space until it's either thrown out or sold at a yard sale for a fraction of what it cost when it was new.

And while this becomes most evident in December, this isn't an issue that's exclusive to that time of year. This is something that surfaces all year long. And what is it evidence of? In my opinion, (and when I say opinion here, I don't really mean opinion because you'd have a hard time convincing me that this isn't fact), but I believe that this is all evidence of deeper level heart issues that aren't being addressed. Let me give you several other examples that I think are related that illustrate the same problem.

Overeating:
When people are overeating, what is that really a sign of? It's not that they love food so much they can't stop consuming it. It's evidence of the fact that they're wrestling with stress or emotional problems that cause them pain. And in a small, temporary way, when they eat food, it brings them momentary comfort or relief of that pain. When they stop eating, they stop feeling that relief, so they eat more and more to avoid having to deal with their pain.

Alcoholism or Drug Addiction:
This is also the case with addiction to substances. How do those addictions take hold? They begin because of a desire to dull feelings of pain. Once they take hold, they become a crutch that is mentally and physically relied on to continue dulling the pain.

Video game addictions:
Video games take their users to other worlds. They can be fun diversions, but sometimes their usage become an addiction when the pain of real life is so strong that the person chooses to check out of the pain of their day-to-day reality through overly using video games.

Relationship addictions:
This happens in relationships as well. People become addicted to the euphoria of a relationship and then, when that wears off, they're reminded of the pain of loneliness that they were relying on that relationship to relieve them of. If the relationship grows stale or if the other person leaves, they immediately move on to a new relationship to relieve the pain.

Financial issues often operate in the same way and those who serve in leadership need to be particularly careful about them. When you're serving in leadership, there are going to be days when you will feel drained. You may feel lonely, stressed, anxious, unappreciated and tired. There are healthy ways to deal with those feelings, but there are also unhealthy ways you can respond.

You can overeat, develop a substance addiction, spend all your time trying to mentally escape or even try to recapture the euphoria of a new relationship as a diversion from your pain, but all those options produce unhealthy results that result in MORE pain. You can also try to satisfy your pain by spending, consuming and accumulating debt, but all that does is set you up for additional pain somewhere down the road.

I had to learn this the hard way. I'm 40 and at present, the only debt I have is my mortgage. It is 10 years away from being paid off, but I hope to pay it off sooner. I don't owe money on student loans, credit cards or vehicles. I have no other debt other than that mortgage and I'm grateful that this is the case, but this hasn't always been the case.

I used to have two mortgages, student debt, tens of thousands of dollars in credit card debt and vehicle loans on cars that I bought brand new. My credit rating has always been perfect. I never missed a payment on anything I owed, but for years, I was living on the very edge of my finances. I was one catastrophe or surprise away from financial ruin.

Why was this the case? Well, there's a variety of things that contributed, but one of the things was the fact that I was very highly stretched and stressed as a leader and buying nice things temporarily dulled the pain. It also put me on a path where I wasn't making wise use of my money. Instead of using my money to earn more money and give generously, I was using my money to buy nice things before I could truly afford to do so. I was trying to live like I was at a season of life that I wasn't really at yet.

Part of that was using my credit cards to finance several business ventures that weren't all worth their cost in the long run. I don't blame myself for trying to be entrepreneurial, but if I could go back to that time, I would have done things differently.

Then, because I was so busy with my leadership roles, I barely had time to sit down and address this problem. I floated month to month, realizing that I needed to get my finances in order, but never sitting down and taking time to get it all figured out.

Finally, after realizing that this was one of the things that I needed to create some space in my life to deal with, I chose to stop serving in some of the roles of leadership I had been serving it. I decided to limit it, for a time, to just one role. Then I made some good decisions regarding my finances that my family has been benefitting from ever since. I upped the level of financial leadership I was providing for my household by doing several things.

1. I figured out exactly how much debt I had

2. The interest rates were high, so I consolidated it all to one card with one low rate.

3. I had three vehicles, but I only needed two, so I sold one and used the money from it to pay down my debts. I traded another on a much cheaper, but still reliable vehicle which saved me about $400 per month between payments and insurance. I used the extra money toward paying down my debts.

4. I became much more intentional and careful

about what I was consuming.

5. I stopped taking on additional debt and stopped using credit cards to make every day purchases. I use a debit card instead. That way I'm only buying things I actually have the money for.

6. I used just about every penny of extra money I had to pay off my debts until they were all gone (except the mortgage, but I'm paying extra on that).

7. Now that my consumer debts are gone, I use my extra money to invest in my 401k and my IRA's so that when I retire, I actually have something to live on.

8. I created several sources of additional income in addition to my job. (Books, voiceover, speaking, coaching, counseling, and several more). Instead of watching TV at night, I often take an hour and invest that time into one of those extra income streams.

9. I have continued to practice "generosity" by donating 10% of my income to the ministry of our local church. I'm not waiting until my finances are "perfect" for me to develop the habit of generous giving.

This approach has been helpful to me and our family. In fact, my wife regularly thanks me for doing all of this and I certainly am grateful for the fact that she appreciates it all. But this has also had an impact on the organization I lead.

As the pastor of a newly planted church, the financial situation of the church is not yet in a predictable groove. There are seasons when the church honestly doesn't have enough income to be able to pay me. They try their best to be generous, but the reality is that the one area of the budget that has the most flex when things get tight is my salary. And by God's grace, it has all worked out.

The only debt I have is my mortgage and since I now have several additional income streams flowing, I have been able to weather the unpredictable financial nature of my leadership role. I've also noticed that when it's really needed, I believe that God has influenced those additional income streams to flow more freely so that the work of the church can continue without the additional stress that would have been cast on this young organization if I was less intentional about employing wisdom regarding my finances.

So, let me say this. If anything that I have shared in this chapter sounds familiar to you and you want to start addressing your finances from a new perspective, let me be the first to encourage you that you can absolutely get that accomplished. It will probably mean that you'll need to address the stress and emotional pain you're experiencing then create some space for you to make an honest assessment of your finances.

Get aggressive about getting rid of things that drain your finances so you can be equally aggressive about clearing up debt. Consider how you might be able to turn your hobbies into sources of income and realize that even though these changes might not happen overnight, they can take place quickly.

You can do this. I'm confident that it will benefit you, your family and the organization that you're leading if you do so.

Further Reading: *I would highly recommend reading **"The Total Money Makeover" by Dave Ramsey** if you're looking for motivation and a plan for improving your financial picture. It's a great book and the advice Dave gives in the book is very helpful. He also hosts a great radio show / podcast that I listen to almost every day.*

Chapter 17

How to lead your organization through seasons of change

Do you enjoy change or do you resist seasons of change in your life? What about the people you're trying to lead? What do they think about change?

When you're in a position of leadership, odds are you're going to have to lead your team or organization through seasons of change. Ironically, even though change is often necessary in every organization, nearly 70% of people have personalities that strongly resist change.

How can you make change more palatable for your team when it's time to make some changes? I'm going to suggest seven ideas on this subject that I think you'll find helpful if you give them a try.

Most leaders would agree that introducing change into an organization can be a very difficult and delicate task. It's not that people don't think that change is necessary from time to time. It's just that, by nature, most people strongly resist change. We prefer the familiar, even if what is familiar no longer makes a lot of sense.

Just think about some of the changes that you have taken a while to adjust to in your life.

1. **New car designs:**
Recently, I was looking at the design updates for one of my favorite car models. I hated them. They looked terrible to me and I can't help but think that others might feel that way too. Yet, after a year or two of seeing this style on the road, I'm sure I'll grow used to it and maybe even end up liking it.

2. **New road patterns:**
The main road near my house has been under construction for over a year. In addition to rebuilding a bridge, they added a traffic circle. I usually hate traffic circles and for a year, I have been whining about that change. Now that it's done, I'm happy about it. It eliminated an awkward right turn and a traffic light I used to get stuck at.

3. **Menus:**
Isn't it the worst when a restaurant you like changes their menu? Especially if they no longer make what you used to get? But then, over time, what happens? We usually find that some of the new things they make taste great and become some of our new favorites.

Change isn't something that we tend to naturally and quickly adjust to. We like the familiar. We like our routines. We like systems that we've grown accustomed to. But healthy organizations aren't organizations that remain stagnant. Stagnancy produces ruts and ruts kill momentum. Healthy organizations are always looking for ways to improve what they are doing and what they can offer.

But what happens if you're trying to lead a group of people and you're encouraging them to support you as you're trying to bring a healthy level of change to your business, organization or church, but you're discovering that they're resistant to change? Keeping in mind that studies show that nearly 70% of people are highly resistant to change, what should you do?

Allow me to make seven suggestions that I think work well if you're trying to lead your organization through a season of change.

1. Talk to key people in your organization first and tell them what you're thinking about doing. It's wise to keep your key leaders informed of your intentions before making general announcements regarding plans and direction for your organization.

2. If the key people in your organization are solid leaders with a strong track record, but they don't support your ideas or your timing, you're going to need to accept that now might not be the right time to press your ideas. You may need to "sell" your idea a little longer or make changes to your original suggestions. It doesn't mean that you will never get to implement your changes. It just means that you're going to need to wait for a better time.

3. When it's time to start implementing change, be upfront with your organization about what you want to do. Most people don't like surprises, so don't surprise them when it comes to things that are going to have a direct impact on them. Be upfront, honest and transparent with them instead.

4. Educate people about why you want to do it. It may be that in some cases, people are resistant to change because the rationale for the change has never been explained to them. If there's something new that needs to be done, you may be operating with more information than many of the others in your organization. Let them know what you know. Grant them access to the big picture that for now, maybe only you can see. Educate your people so they will know why you want to do what you want to do.

5. Give your people time to adapt to new ideas before you implement them. I realize there are some contexts when immediate change is necessary, but in most contexts, change doesn't need to be implemented one second after it has been announced. I have found that in certain contexts, it has been helpful to me to ease people into change by giving them several months advance notice.

I will warn you about one risk that comes with this. Even though you may be doing this for the betterment of the organization you lead, you might experience some pain and pushback during this time of delay and it may feel personal at times. If the change you're trying to implement is for the betterment of the organization, you're just going to have to find a way to deal with the painful pushback and accept it as a temporary reality. This is a time when relying on the encouragement of good friends can be key.

6. Pledge that after giving it enough time to be tested, if what you're doing doesn't work, you'll admit that it's not working and either revert back to the old system or try something different that might

work better. I have found this to be a major help to me when I'm trying to make changes. People are often willing to let you try something as long as you promise not to keep pushing it if it isn't better than the old system. Then, of course, you need to make good on this promise if it doesn't work.

7. Listen to suggestions from your team on how to make additional adaptations to your changes. There are going to be a few ways that what you're doing may need to be tweaked once it's being implemented. When those adaptations are suggested by your team, honor their suggestions. They're the ones who are supporting you and helping you to implement your changes. If they have an idea that can make it even better, don't be afraid to take their suggestions.

This is the approach I take when I'm trying to implement changes and I have found that in my context, it has worked rather well. I take this approach because this is how I prefer to be led. If a leader is about to make changes that will impact me, there is a way I like to be led through those changes and a way that I don't.

I don't appreciate...

Dictatorial leaders:
These are leaders who don't understand that "leadership" and being a "boss" are quite different. Dictatorial personalities strike me as being arrogant and I find that off-putting.

Disorganized leaders:
These are leaders who don't seem to have a plan. They seem more reactive than proactive and I usually feel like they spend too much time putting out fires and not enough time implementing change or creating healthy organizational cultures.

Leaders who can't articulate "why" a change needs to be made:
If you're just making changes for the sake of change, that can get old really quickly. If you can't explain why a change needs to be made, you might want to consider waiting until you can offer that explanation before trying to implement the change because inevitably, the first question you're going to get is, "Why are we doing this?" If you can't give an answer, you're not going to be able to lead the change.

Leaders who can't take suggestions:
Some leaders struggle with an overabundance of pride and insecurity. They want an idea to be exclusively theirs and therefore, they tend to be hesitant to hear and implement suggestions, even if those suggestions are good. I don't appreciate this kind of leadership.

Leaders who won't admit when they're wrong:
We're all wrong sometimes and our people know when we're wrong. We may not want to admit we're wrong because we may fear that that will somehow diminish our ability to lead. But, ironically, the opposite is true. Leaders who can admit that they're wrong actually strengthen the level of trust they receive

from their people. Leaders who won't admit when they're wrong quickly diminish the trust of their team.

If you're in leadership, there are going to be seasons when you'll need to lead your team through change. I believe that if you apply these principles, you'll experience greater success when it's time to make changes.

Every organization experiences the need for change, but it takes a wise leader to navigate those changes well. Be the kind of leader that shows your team and your organization that you value their input, needs and personal contribution while you invite them to join you in making the changes that need to be made for the betterment of the organization as a whole.

Chapter 18

Motivation, appreciation, and being the kind of leader people like working with

In just a few moments, we're going to talk about a combination of related concepts. I'm calling this chapter, "Motivation, appreciation and being the kind of leader people like working with", because I think each of those subjects flow nicely together.

What does it look like to motivate your team?

How can you show the people you lead genuine appreciation?

How does this relate to being the kind of leader people like working with? Please notice that I'm saying "working with" as opposed to saying "working for." I think these concepts start right there with that distinction.

As I have shared many times already and I'll share many times more, being a leader is much different from being a boss. It's a completely different mindset. A leader considers himself the navigator of a team. He has influence over a group of people that trust his ability to make decisions and he considers himself to be part of the team. He isn't merely over the team. He's part of it. A boss, on the other hand, considers himself above the team and is probably correct in assuming that the people he's trying to lead don't consider him part of the team.

It is more rewarding to work <u>with</u> a leader who considers himself part of the team than it is to work <u>for</u> a boss that considers himself over the team.

When you're part of a team, you share victories. You share successes. You share wins and you root for each other. When you're over a team, you're probably more bent on punishing failures than you are focused on giving credit for success. In fact, I have noticed that good leaders tend to be generous in sharing the credit for success with their team while bosses tend to direct credit toward themselves and place blame on those they oversee when things don't go as planned.

Leaders create a sense of belonging and long-term loyalty. Bosses create environments that people want to leave because they feel demeaned and devalued.

A few months ago, I received a message from someone who used to be part of my leadership team when I was leading the Pocono Mountain Bible Conference. At that time, she was part of my inner circle of leadership and she worked with me for several years until she moved to a different part of the country.

Her message encouraged me. This is what she said:

> *I am currently taking a class in nursing school called "Professional Practice and Leadership." I have always admired your ability to lead people, and it's something I don't think I'm particularly good at. I tend to expect too much from people, and they get frustrated. But you seem able to keep good morale while still requiring people to meet high standards.*

You don't happen to have written a book on this topic, do you? If not, is it something that interests you? Something along the lines of Biblical management style? I'm hoping to become a nurse practitioner in the future, and I would love to have some tips!

Like I said, I was encouraged to read this message from someone that worked with me in leadership for several years, and I will also say that she's a much better leader than she gives herself credit for. I loved the way she helped lead our team and the quality oversight she gave to our program at PMBC.

My question for her or for anyone who might be experiencing a sense that their team is more frustrated than motivated is to look at the culture surrounding your team. If you're operating as a leader and navigator, you're essentially inviting a group of people to trust you and go on a journey or adventure with you. That's the mindset you want to convey. You may not know all the outcomes of the journey ahead of time, but you're inviting them to come with you to find out what lies ahead.

If you're operating as a boss, you're telling them to go on a journey without you, while demanding that they send you regular updates and expense reports so that you can micromanage the details of their trip, even though you're not part of the journey they're taking. In that case, you're not leading a team, you're giving orders to a group of subordinates.

Creating a team culture, in my estimation, is much better and more fruitful to the mission of your organization than creating a culture populated by bosses and subordinates.

But let's take this a step further. Let's say you've created that team culture and you're a leader that people generally like to work with. What can you do to keep motivation high and how can you actively show appreciation to your team?

To be honest, I don't think this is an easy question to answer, and if your answer to this question differs from mine, I would love for you to send me an email, but I do have a few thoughts that I think work well and I want to point you to an unconventional source for some inspiration.

In the mid 1990's, Gary Chapman wrote a book titled, *"The Five Love Languages."* It's a book that I often recommend for married couples and it outlines five primary ways people tend to show love toward others or receive love from others. The five ways that he lists are, *words of affirmation, quality time, physical touch, acts of service and gifts.*

When couples take time to identify the primary love language of their spouse, they can make regular investments in that area that will help their spouse to feel loved. I tend to be a *"words of affirmation"* guy, so when my wife says something encouraging to me, it makes me feel loved. She tends to be a *"quality time"* kind of person. So when I carve time out to spend with her, it makes her feel loved. Somewhere along the way, it dawned on me that this practice also goes a long way toward helping the people I lead feel appreciated.

We all tend to show love and appreciation in the ways that we want to receive love and appreciation, so I have a natural tendency to verbally praise people, but that's not everyone's love language. Since coming to that realization, I have made a practice of trying to figure out the love languages of the teams I lead. I don't usually ask them directly, because I think that would be kind of weird. *"So, um, Vince, can you tell me what your primary love language is?"* Yeah, I don't do it like that.

But I have found that you can usually figure out what a person's love language is just by observing what they tend to do. If they tend to bring cookies to work to share, they might be a gift giver. Make a note of that. If you want to encourage that person, they'll probably appreciate a gift from time to time - even something as small as a candy bar or a new pen. If they tend to engage you in lengthy conversations, they might be a quality time person. Write that down and invite them to join you for lunch sometime. They will feel appreciated by your investment of your time in them. If they tend to compliment you or others, they're probably a words of affirmation person. If you make a point to remember that, you can encourage that person with verbal or written words of encouragement. You get the idea.

The only one that I struggle with is the physical touch people. That's almost always a bad idea in a work environment. We all know awkward huggers and we probably lead a few. Most likely, they show love to others and feel loved by others when they receive physical touch. I would strongly advise that you not give them a back rub at work or brush their hair for them. I guess you can try using the awkward side hug option, but for the most part, I would advise not showing appreciation to these people. They're not worth having on your team anyway. They're always going to be in your space and that gets annoying.

Of course I'm kidding, but you'll need to use extra discernment if you're trying to show people appreciation when they're physical touch kind of people. In that case, you might want to see if you can discern what their secondary love language might be and then go with that one.

All in all, what you're trying to do is to create a culture that lets your team know that you're together with them on this journey and that you genuinely appreciate the skills, gifts and talents they bring to your organization. A little bit of intentionality in this department can go a long way toward keeping motivation high and frustration low.

Chapter 19

Questions and answers for young leaders

Are you a new leader or someone who is relatively young and you're serving in a role of leadership, possibly for the first time? If so, you probably have a few questions.

From time to time, I receive calls, texts and emails from new and young leaders that I consider friends. I appreciate new and young leaders and the energy, optimism and enthusiasm they bring to an organization. As we prepare to conclude this book, I thought it might be helpful to include some of those questions as well as a few answers. Hopefully, even if you're a seasoned leader, you'll find this chapter helpful.

---

1. **"For young leaders, how do you recommend finding opportunities to mentor others?"**

First of all, let me commend this leader's desire to mentor others. I believe that good leaders make a point to mentor other leaders. I think that's a big part of healthy leadership, the replication and multiplication of leaders. Mentoring is a sacrifice of a leader's time, but it's a healthy sacrifice and it often has a noticeable dual benefit, both to the leader and the person that is being mentored. It provides a creative outlet for the leader and can even be useful for helping a leader clarify his thinking or his approach.

Now, if you're a young leader and you have the desire to mentor others, that's a great thing and this question had to do with where to find people to mentor. From my experience, what I see as a typical pattern is that leaders usually find themselves mentoring or investing their time in those who are one or more seasons behind them in their service and they may already have some level of involvement in your organization.

In my case, I frequently have found myself mentoring people who, on average are about 10-20 years younger than me. There are a few exceptions to that, but generally, that's who I have been most commonly working with in a mentoring kind of role.

So I would say that if you know people one season behind you, maybe 5 or 10 years younger than you that have a desire to serve in a similar leadership capacity as you, I would start with them, particularly if they tend to seek your opinion and guidance already.

---

2. "As a leader, how do you decide if it's worth stepping into a situation to prevent someone underneath you from failing, or to let them fail in order to learn a lesson?"

That's a great question and not an easy question to answer. To some degree, I would say the answer to that question depends on the teachability of the person you're trying to help and your own motives in choosing to help someone or let them fail.

Some people are enjoyable to work with and they show a lot of promise and potential. If their intentions are good and they maintain a teachable spirit, they will frequently find people going out of their way to help them out and likewise people will probably take an interest in looking out for their best interests. It is a joy to invest your time and energy in the lives of teachable people.

Then there are those who aren't teachable at all. They already think they know everything and after a few attempts to help them, you may discover that they aren't interested in hearing what you have to say or acting on the suggestions you have offered them. Eventually that will catch up to them, but because they lack the wisdom and maturity to learn things the easy way by accepting the counsel of others, they will unfortunately have to learn the hard way by making painful and costly mistakes that could have been avoided.

When you encounter people like that who rebuff your attempts to help them, sometimes the best thing you can do for them is to let them learn the hard way. But be merciful in this process. There are some bad decisions that have worse consequences than others. If they're about to make a decision that has long-term harmful consequences for them or for the organization you're part of, I would still probably try to step into the situation even if they aren't very teachable. But if the consequences aren't that severe, it might be worth stepping back a little and letting their experiences do the work of tenderizing their hearts a little.

> **Proverbs 9:8** speaks to this subject and says this, *"So don't bother correcting mockers; they will only hate you. But correct the wise, and they will love you."*

---

3. "What are the top three books you would recommend for aspiring leaders?"

Here's my answer and my rationale for each.

1. *"The 21 Irrefutable Laws of Leadership" by John Maxwell* is a fantastic book for breaking down the essence of some of the major, universal principles of leadership. It's an easy book to read, but it's content is meaningful and practical. I read it to my children, out loud, regularly, partly for their benefit, but also for mine. It's filled with great stories and examples and I think you'll find it helpful.

2. Another book that is one of my personal favorites is called, *"Lincoln on Leadership" by Donald T. Phillips*. The book takes a look at what made Abraham Lincoln such an effective leader during a pivotal time in American history. I found the book to be insightful and I have taken a lot of encouragement from it.

3. The third book I would recommend is really two books and it won't surprise anyone that this is on my list of recommendations. But I think all leaders should make themselves acquainted with the books of *Psalms and Proverbs from the Bible.*

In the book of Psalms, you have multiple psalmists, but primarily King David, pouring out his heart and soul regarding what his life as a leader was like. He trusted in God in the midst of difficult seasons of leadership and he gives us a glimpse into his heart as he did so.

The book of Proverbs was primarily written by David's

son, Solomon, who also served as a king and within the pages of that book, there are scores of insightful thoughts related to the character of leaders and the way human nature truly works. I consider both biblical books indispensable tools in my leadership.

---

4. "Can you shed some light on tips for leading people that are significantly more experienced or older than you?"

I like that question because that has been something I have had to deal with throughout the course of my adult life. In fact, some of you may already know that I was first hired as a full-time pastor when I was fresh out of college at age 21. That didn't feel particularly young to me at the time, but now it does and I will admit that during that season of life, l often felt a little timid about trying to lead at such a young age.

Here are a few tips:

1. Stop telling yourself how young you are and don't overly focus on how you come across to others. Rather, focus on providing value for those you're called to lead and welcome the ways in which they try to provide value to you. In some respects, I have found it helpful to treat them with the kind of respect I always had for my grandparents. My grandparents acknowledged that there were certain things that I knew and could bring to the table and I honored their wisdom, experience and assistance.

2. Don't be afraid to admit when you're wrong. It won't diminish your ability to lead. It will actually help you to build trust and respect.

3. Live and serve in such a way that you're doing your job in a way that demonstrates your character and commitment. There's a Bible verse that speaks to this as well. The Apostle Paul mentored Timothy who was a rather young pastor and it appears that Timothy found his leadership role rather intimidating at times. This is what Paul said to Timothy in **1 Timothy 4:12**, *"Don't let anyone think less of you because you are young. Be an example to all believers in what you say, in the way you live, in your love, your faith, and your purity."*

Wrapping Up

When most people buy a book, there is a part of them that thinks that because they now own the book, they will benefit from it's content. But a book needs to be read and applied for it to become truly useful. If you have successfully read this book to the end, please allow me to be the first to applaud you. You have made an intentional investment in your leadership and I hope that will be a true help to you and to those who live and serve under your leadership.

That being said, let me encourage you to continue making investments in your leadership. Keep learning. Keep serving. Keep surrounding yourself with people who lift you up, value you and motivate you to continue serving in the trenches of whatever field, organization or ministry you're serving.

Leadership isn't easy, but it's important. There is a deficit of good leaders in this world and I hope that by God's grace, He will enable you to lead others with a servant's heart that truly reflects the heart of Jesus.

Your fellow servant,
John Stange

Contact the Author

John Stange can be reached via his website: DesireJesus.com

www.ingramcontent.com/pod-product-compliance
Lightning Source LLC
Chambersburg PA
CBHW060347190526
45169CB00002B/514